Your
Samoyed

By Jan Kauzlarich

Compiled and Edited by
William W. Denlinger and R. Annabel Rathman

Cover design by
Bruce Parker

DENLINGER'S
Box 76, Fairfax, Virginia 22030

Reproduced on the front cover of this book is a head study of Ch. Nachalnik of Drayalene (Ch. Rokandi of Drayalene x Clarisse of Drayalene). Now deceased, "Chiefie" was owned by Harold and Doris McLaughlin of Morrison, Colorado. One of the great Samoyeds of all time, he won the Samoyed Club of America Stud Dog Trophy in 1970, 1973, and 1974, and holds the record for producing thirty-five American champion sons and daughters to date.

Reproduced on the back cover is a photograph of the Samoyed team of Bob and Wanda Krauss, sledding on the ice of Lake Mendota near Madison, Wisconsin. In double lead on the right is Ch. K-Way's Gay Gazelle and at the left is Prairiewind's Little Cindy, CD; at right swing is Aeolius Chinook, CD, and at left swing is K-Way's Garmouche, CD; at right wheel is K-Way's Silver Solitaire, CD, and at left wheel is Ch. Prairiewind's Shanna, CD.

The Author with two of her dogs, Kauzja Cheefatu (on left) and Cheefatu's uncle, Kauzja Azzagai.

Foreword

Why would anybody want to own a dog, anyway?

In the beginning, dogs were man's partners in hunting expeditions and acted as camp guards and drivers of stock; and sometimes they still do these useful jobs. In today's urbanized society, dogs are still valued; but their main job seems to be as companions to man.

Man is the only animal who keeps other animals as companions, as pets. No chimpanzee, however advanced, ever kept canaries. This keeping of pets is behavior that sets man apart, and seems to fill a very deep-seated, strong drive in man. The need fulfilled by pets is the innate human drive to nurture and rear the human infant. Pets are child-substitutes. Being gregarious and cooperating animals like man himself, dogs make superb human-infant substitutes.

That statement is likely to make dog-owning unmarried individuals and childless couples uncomfortable. However, as a dog breeder, I have found that the majority of the puppies I sell go into homes with children—and as pets for the adults, not the children, in the family. One couple with three children told me frankly that they had been considering having another baby, but decided to buy a dog instead! And I suspect that the increase in the dog population in this country is due as much to the recent trend in limiting the size of families as to the rise of urban crime figures and the acquisition of new status symbols.

So why would anyone want to own a Samoyed?

An extremely ancient Arctic breed, the Samoyed first joined man as a hunter and a guard. His initial appeal to the modern dog owner is the look and feel of his thick, sparkling white coat which is the product of natural selection, as is the white coat of other Arctic creatures. The Samoyed's coat requires special attention, and that should be given some consideration before anyone buys his first Samoyed. The Samoyed's most lasting appeal is his distinctive personality. He is a most companionable dog, friendly and delighted to spend his time with humans, but with a dash of strong, primitive pepper. This also is a product of natural selection in the Arctic.

This book is designed to provide the new Samoyed owner with some of the history and background of the breed as well as to serve as an aid in routine care and maintenance; and, most importantly, to help him love and enjoy his Samoyed to the fullest extent.

My special thanks to Mrs. John Chittum for her invaluable help in the preparation of the material on the spinning and weaving of Samoyed hair included in the chapter on the Samoyed coat; to Mrs. Joseph Marineau, Mrs. Carl Chiono, and my husband for reading and commenting on the manuscript; and to all the Samoyed fanciers whom I called upon and who furnished the pictures which illustrate this book.

To new Samoyed owners and prospective owners, a good luck and a word of warning—Sammies are addictive.

J.K.

Ch. Sno Kandi's Hondo of Drayalene, one of the top ten winning Samoyeds for 1966. Owners, Walt and Jan Kauzlarich.

The consistently winning Samoyed team trained and driven by Pat Enslen, pictured at the 1976 races at Squaw Valley in the Sierra Nevadas. In double lead are Blanca Rena of Snow Ridge and Whitecliff's General Custer. Visible at wheel is Ch. Winter Frost of Whitecliff, eight years of age and the sire of General Custer and Shana of Whitecliff, the swing dog at the left.

Contents

Selecting a Samoyed Puppy   9
The Adult Samoyed   15
     Standard of the Samoyed   17
The Samoyed Coat   23
     How to Make Use of All That Hair   29
Grooming the Family Dog   33
"Bed and Board" for the Family Dog   37
Maintaining the Dog's Health   43
History of the Genus *Canis*   57
History of the Samoyed   65
The Samoyed in America   71
Samoyed Club of American Trophy Winners   87
     Top Winning Samoyed Dog   87
     Top Winning Samoyed Bitch   88
     Top Producing Samoyed Stud Dog   88
     Top Producing Samoyed Brood Bitch   89
     Top Obedience Samoyed   89
     Samoyed Club of America Specialty Best of Breed
          Winners   91
A Very Special Personality   93
The Samoyed as a Working Dog   99
Manners for the Family Dog   105
Show Competition   113
Genetics   125
Breeding and Whelping   131

Between seven and ten weeks of age, a Samoyed will look much as he will at three years of age. This puppy is more than a darling ball of fluff. Notice the long neck, the good substance in the bones of his feet and legs, the broad head and muzzle, and how he stands well up on all four legs. As he grows he will be a naughty, noisy, destructive rascal—a typical Samoyed.

Selecting a Samoyed Puppy

The future owner of a Samoyed falls in love with a darling white, fluffy, black-eyed puppy that looks for all the world like a cuddly stuffed toy. But a Samoyed is not a dog to sit quietly on a shelf. He is going to grow into a sixty-five pound ball of fur which periodically sheds out, has strong primitive instincts, and is clever, independent, demanding, and full of energy and vitality. He is not a dog for everybody—least of all for the person who wants a stuffed-toy kind of dog!

It is best to visit with adult Samoyeds and their owners before making up your mind to buy a puppy. When you have decided that you are the person to own a smart, sassy kind of dog and that the care of the long coat is not going to bother you, it will be time to go hunting for that adorable puppy.

The place to go is the kennel of an experienced, reputable breeder. You will need lessons in grooming and help in rearing your puppy, whether you want a pet or a show dog. Buying your puppy from such a breeder will guarantee that you have a pure-bred, registered dog. Be prepared to answer questions about your home and life style, for a reputable breeder will want to know whether you are the right person to be a Samoyed owner.

The experienced breeder shows his dogs, and he will be honest with you about the strong and weak points of his bloodlines and whether the puppy is pet quality or show stock. Show stock is usually reserved before the parents are even bred, so if you are interested in a puppy for showing, be prepared to wait and to pay top price for him.

In buying a show puppy, do not be blinded by the flashy wins of the parents, for some of the greatest show dogs are indifferent producers. Look instead to the bloodlines that consistently produce quality animals that are uniform in soundness and beauty. This holds true for pet stock as well. A pet puppy from a top show litter is going to be a better adult than the best puppy in a pets-only litter.

9

These seven-week-old puppies already have their ears up. They are keeping themselves entertained by wrestling and playing. A solitary Samoyed puppy must always have a large collection of toys to play with.

Samoyeds make excellent pets for children. Here twelve-year-old Lisa Klambrum is seen with seven-week-old Rickshaw's Ksunji of Kalmarli. Ksunji is now an adult dog, trained and handled in the show ring by his young owner.

Beware the breeder who says his dogs are without faults. There is no perfect dog in any breed! Shop around among breeders in your area, and, if possible, attend a few dog shows. A Samoyed is a long-lived dog and will be with you for twelve to fourteen years. You can afford to invest some time visiting breeders before you make a purchase.

Do not hesitate to buy a puppy four to six months old. He is growing out of the cute stage into the leggy, gawky stage, but he is also housebroken. His inoculations are completed, and he is through the worst chewing stage. A puppy of this age is the answer for the person who works because he can be left alone during the day provided he has a run or other safe place and has plenty of toys to keep him entertained. A Sam should never have the run of the house while his owner is away—unless you do not mind having your household goods chewed up.

A good investment is a large wire crate. It can double as a dog bed and as a safe place if your dog travels with you. It is also a good place to keep an active puppy for an hour or two while you are shopping. If your Samoyed is going to be left alone for the entire day, he should have a large pen in the garage or his own run in the back yard.

Samoyeds are subject to two common problems. One is a flighty, over-excitable temperament; the other is hip dysplasia, a deformity of the hip joints. Both are hereditary, but the breeding stock of a reputable breeder has been selected away from these traits. Parents of puppies should be x-rayed and should be certified clear of hip dysplasia by the Orthopedic Foundation for Animals and assigned an O.F.A. number. The parents should also have been checked and cleared of the eye problem called progressive retinal atrophy, which leads to blindness. It is not a widespread problem in Samoyeds, but good breeding stock is checked for it.

A Samoyed matures slowly, so a puppy is rarely weaned before six weeks of age. He needs to learn to socialize properly with his own kind and can develop quirks of temperament if removed from the litter before seven weeks of age. Never buy a Samoyed puppy younger than that.

In most cases the breeder will select your puppy for you. But if you are allowed to choose, look for the puppy that is bright eyed and lively and stands up on his toes with his tail over his back. He should enjoy being cuddled and petted, and should respond with interest to unusual noises. His coat should be thick and full with a healthy feel to it. The dewclaws must be removed from the rear legs. Some breeders also remove the dewclaws from the front legs, which is best but not essential.

The head and muzzle should be broad and blunt with the eyes slanting upward from the outer corners toward the outer base of the ears. The lip line in profile should be curved and tight at the corners, giving the characteristic Samoyed "smile" and expression. At seven or eight weeks of age, the ears may not be fully erect, but they should be at least halfway up, with the base thick and sturdy. Puppies from some bloodlines are slower about developing stiff cartilage in their ears, and if the puppy's ears are still floppy, discuss the problem with the breeder. Sometimes in an extremely furry puppy, the added weight of the coat prevents the ears from standing and it will be necessary to trim the hair from the ears. Ears should be erect by ten weeks of age.

The body of the puppy should be firm and thrifty, and he should be slightly longer in back than he is tall at the shoulders. His neck should be long. The bones of his legs should be thick and have a "fat" look, and his paws should look bigger in proportion to his size than an adult dog's would.

The puppy should have had the inoculations appropriate for his age, which would be distemper, hepatitis, and leptospirosis for a young dog. For an older puppy, rabies should be included. All puppies get round worms, but the appropriate wormings should have been started. Some areas are badly infested with heartworms, so discuss this problem with the breeder and your veterinarian.

Avoid a puppy that is shy or overaggressive, or is terrified of loud noises. Also avoid a puppy with runny eyes, dull, brittle coat, swollen potty belly, or rank breath. Do not select a puppy with round, bulgy eyes or a break in the black pigmentation around the eyes, spindly bones in the legs, short legs, or a coarse face.

The reputable breeder will furnish you with written instructions on grooming, and on nutrition for your dog both as a puppy and as an adult. Because Samoyeds have special nutritional needs, you should follow the instructions closely. It is much easier adapting to the demands of a new puppy if you collect your equipment before you bring him home. You will need a water and food dish—preferably stainless steel, for a Sam will make short work of a plastic dish. You will need to decide where he is going to sleep and to prepare his bed, preferably a metal crate. No mattress is necessary, for Samoyeds provide their own. You will need some chew toys, a soft hair brush for puppy grooming, and a soft puppy lead.

It you live within driving distance of the kennel, you will want someone to accompany you to help with the puppy in the car. If your puppy is being shipped to you, it is customary for the new owner to pay the shipping costs. Puppies should not be shipped air freight under three months of age, for the trauma and stress are much too great for a younger puppy.

If you decide to buy a puppy from a breeder outside your area and will get the puppy sight unseen, beware of fancy advertising. Spend some time corresponding with the breeder and ask for pictures of his dogs and kennels. Also, check out the breeder's reputation with the members of the local breed club. An experienced breeder will know other experienced breeders throughout the country as well as the relative merits of their dogs and breeding programs. He may be a bit "catty" about other breeders' show stock, but he can definitely inform you as to the state of their kennels and the care they give their dogs.

At the time you buy the puppy, an ethical breeder will provide you with a five or six generation pedigree of your puppy. The breeder will also give you an American Kennel Club "blue slip" which he has signed and which you must have in order to register your dog with The American Kennel Club. You will enter your first and second choice of a name for your puppy, the date of purchase, and your signature, and send the blue slip plus a small fee to The American Kennel Club. In return the A.K.C. will send you a white registration slip with your dog's official registered name and A.K.C. number. This is your dog's "papers."

When choosing a name for a Samoyed, new owners are often inspired by the dog's white coat, and, as a result, there are thousands of Samoyeds named "Frosty" and "Snowy." The breed is of Russian origin, and Russian language given names or place names make good Samoyed names. Also, a name derived from the owner's name makes a good name for a Samoyed.

Any breeder worth his salt will insist that you take your puppy to your veterinarian for an immediate health check. The breeder will also provide you with a health record to give to your veterinarian.

The name of this breed is the most mispronounced in dogdom! The correct pronunciation is "Sam ee add," with the accent on the last syllable so that it rhymes with "Come and add."

13

Ch. Snowline's Joli Shashan, CDX, owned by Tom and Mary Mayfield and bred by Skip and Nancy Alexander. Besides a top career in the conformation ring, Shawnie was the Samoyed Club of America top obedience dog for 1969.

Ch. Belaya's Anja Padrushka, a top winning California Samoyed and champion-producing brood bitch owned and handled by John and Carol Chittum.

Ch. Kondako's Dancing Bear, 1972 Samoyed Club of America top producing stud dog. Bred, owned, and handled by Dave and Connie Richardson.

The Adult Samoyed

The Samoyed is a Working Dog. Primarily a guard dog and hunting dog for large game, he was also used as a sled dog and for driving the herds by his original owners, the Samoyede people of Northern Europe. As an all-purpose Working Dog, his body and running gear are of the utmost importance and he must be built for stamina as well as for speed and agility. A Samoyed has great beauty while he is standing or lying quietly at your feet, but he should also have beauty in motion, a kinesthetic beauty which is not dependent on whether he is in or out of coat. This beauty in motion is a flowing, smooth, well-coordinated trot that eats up the distance. A Samoyed should be able to go all day without exhaustion, and after a good night's sleep he should be ready to go the next day. The owner of a Samoyed never has to worry about his dog becoming footsore, for the Samoyed has an unusually tough foot with thick pads and strong, thick nails that will take lots of wear.

Much has been written in literature on the breed about the "bear" head and the "wolf" head. There are really three types of Samoyed head: the "bear," which has a very broad skull and a very broad, blunt muzzle; the "wolf," which has a longer, narrower, and more tapered muzzle; and the type in between these two extremes, which is the proper Samoyed head. Type of head is strictly a matter of personal preference, although dogs with the "wolf" type heads tend to have the best gait. There are two elements of the Samoyed head that are of the utmost importance. One is a deep-set, upward-slanting, almond-shaped eye; the other is the profile of the lip line, which should be curved upward, with lips tight and firm at the corners. If either of these elements is missing, the characteristic Samoyed expression is lost, so always avoid a Sammy with round "buggy" eyes or floppy lips.

Like all Arctic breeds, Samoyeds have voracious appetites and extremely efficient digestive systems, so nearly all pet Samoyeds are overweight and the majority are obese. Excess weight is the number one health problem in the breed. It is an ailment caused

15

Top winning
Samoyed of all
time, American,
Canadian, and
Bermudian Ch.
Lulhaven's Snow-
mist Ensign. Own-
ers, Ott Hyatt and
Sonny White.

by owners—they just simply overfeed their dogs. It is easy to do, for Sams always act as if they are starving to death and are the most expert beggers in dogdom. In planning meals for your adult Samoyed, cut his portions to sixty percent of what another dog his size should be fed. This maintenance diet will keep a plump, healthy adult Samoyed. Remembering that the breed was developed in a sparse, Arctic environment where one mouthful had to go a long way, note that the Samoyed's environment has changed to one of abundance but his digestive system is still geared to the tundras. Cater to that digestive system, not to his charming begging.

The Samoyed is commonly thought to be a pure white dog, but he usually has some spot of light tan, called "biscuit," or even a black hair or two some place in his coat. The biscuit coloring is most commonly found on the backs of the ears. Sometimes a Sam will have biscuit freckles on his muzzle or legs, or even a biscuit patch on his body. This coloring is desirable, for breeders have found that the best coats are produced by individuals with some biscuit coloring, and the touch of off-white adds character to the coat.

The first American Standard for the Samoyed was adopted by the Samoyed Club of America and The American Kennel Club in 1923. In the late 1950s, breeders felt a revised and more refined Standard was needed. The present Standard was prepared and in 1963 was approved by The American Kennel Club. This is the ideal by which all Samoyeds are judged today.

STANDARD OF THE SAMOYED

General Conformation—(a) *General Appearance*—The Samoyed, being essentially a working dog, should present a picture of beauty, alertness and strength, with agility, dignity and grace. As his work lies in cold climates, his coat should be heavy and weather resistant, well groomed, and of good quality rather than quantity. The male carries more of a "ruff" than the female. He should not be long in the back as a weak back would make him practically useless for his legitimate work, but at the same time, a close-coupled body would also place him at a great disadvantage as a draft dog. Breeders should aim for the happy medium, a body not long but muscular, allowing liberty, with a deep chest and well-sprung ribs, strong neck, straight front and especially strong loins. Males should be masculine in appearance and deportment without unwarranted aggressiveness; bitches feminine without weakness of structure or apparent softness of temperament. Bitches may be slightly longer in back than males. They should both give the appearance of being capable of great endurance but be free from coarseness. Because of the depth of chest required, the legs should be moderately long. A very short-legged dog is to be deprecated. Hindquarters should be particularly well developed, stifles well bent and any suggestion of unsound stifles or cowhocks severely penalized. General appearance should include movement and general conformation, indicating balance and good substance.

(b) *Substance*—Substance is that sufficiency of bone and muscle which rounds out a balance with the frame. The bone is heavier than would be expected in a dog of this size but not so massive as to prevent the speed and agility most desirable in a Samoyed. In all builds, bone should be in proportion to body size. The Samoyed should never be so heavy as to appear clumsy nor so light as to appear racy. The weight should be in proportion to the height.

(c) *Height*—Males—21 to 23½ inches; female—19 to 21 inches at the withers. An oversized or undersized Samoyed is to be penalized according to the extent of the deviation.

(d) *Coat* (Texture and Condition)—The Samoyed is a double-coated dog. The body should be well covered with an undercoat of soft, short, thick, close wool with longer and harsh hair growing through it to form the outer coat, which stands straight out from the body and should be free from curl. The coat should form a ruff around the neck and shoulders, framing the head (more on males than on females). Quality of coat should be weather resistant and considered more than quantity. A droopy coat is undesirable. The coat should glisten with a silver sheen. The female does not usually carry as long a coat as most males and it is softer in texture.

(e) *Color*—Samoyeds should be pure white, white and biscuit, cream, or all biscuit. Any other colors disqualify.

Movement—(a) *Gait*—The Samoyed should trot, not pace. He should move with a quick agile stride that is well timed. The gait should be free, balanced and vigorous, with good reach in the forequarters and good driving power in the hindquarters. When trotting, there should be a strong rear action drive. Moving at a slow walk or trot, they will not single track, but as speed increases the legs gradually angle inward until the pads are finally falling on a line directly under the longitudinal center of the body. As the pad marks converge the forelegs and hind legs are carried straight forward in traveling, the stifles not turned in nor out. The back should remain strong, firm and level. A choppy or stilted gait should be penalized.

Ch. White Krystal's Balalika, lead dog of the racing team of Dutch and Lenore Sprock, who are active members of the Sierra-Nevada Dog Drivers Association.

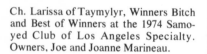

Ch. Larissa of Taymylyr, Winners Bitch and Best of Winners at the 1974 Samoyed Club of Los Angeles Specialty. Owners, Joe and Joanne Marineau.

Best-in-Show winning Ch. Pushka Czar of Snowcliff, one of the top ten winning Samoyeds for three consecutive years. Owned by Randy and Lois Wendelin and handled by twelve-year-old Lori Wendelin.

(b) *Rear End*—Upper thighs should be well developed. Stifles well bent—approximately 45 degrees to the ground. Hocks should be well developed, sharply defined and set at approximately 30 per cent of hip height. The hind legs should be parallel when viewed from the rear in a natural stance, strong, well developed, turning neither in nor out. Straight stifles are objectionable. Double jointedness or cowhocks are a fault. Cowhocks should only be determined if the dog has had an opportunity to move properly.

(c) *Front End*—Legs should be parallel and straight to the pasterns. The pasterns should be strong, sturdy and straight, but flexible with some spring for proper let-down of feet. Because of depth of chest, legs should be moderately long. Length of leg from the ground to the elbow should be approximately 55 per cent of the total height at the withers—a very short-legged dog is to be deprecated. Shoulders should be long and sloping, with a layback of 45 degrees and be firmly set. Out at the shoulders or out at the elbows should be penalized. The withers separation should be approximately 1-1½ inches.

(d) *Feet*—Large, long, flattish—a hare-foot, slightly spread but not splayed; toes arched; pads thick and tough, with protective growth of hair between the toes. Feet should turn neither in nor out in a natural stance but may turn in slightly in the act of pulling. Turning out, pigeon-toed, round or cat-footed or splayed are faults. Feathers on feet are not too essential but are more profuse on females than on males.

Head—(a) *Conformation*–Skull is wedge-shaped, broad, slightly crowned, not round or apple-headed, and should form an equilateral triangle on lines between the inner base of the ears and the center point of the stop. *Muzzle*—Muzzle of medium length and medium width, neither coarse nor snipy; should taper toward the nose and be in proportion to the size of the dog and the width of skull. The muzzle must have depth. *Stop*—Not too abrupt, nevertheless well defined. *Lips*—Should be black for preference and slightly curved up at the corners of the mouth, giving the "Samoyed smile." Lip lines should not have the appearance of being coarse nor should the flews drop predominately at corners of the mouth.

Ears—Strong and thick, erect, triangular and slightly rounded at the tips; should not be large or pointed, nor should they be small and "bear-eared." Ears should conform to head size and the size of the dog; they should be set well apart but be within the border of the outer edge of the head; they should be mobile and well covered inside with hair; hair full and stand-off before the ears. Length of ear should be the same measurement as the distance from inner base of ear to outer corner of eye.

Eyes—Should be dark for preference; should be placed well apart and deep-set; almond shaped with lower lid slanting toward an imaginary point approximating the base of ears. Dark eye rims for preference. Round or protruding eyes penalized. Blue eyes disqualifying.

Nose—Black for preference but brown, liver, or Dudley nose not penalized. Color of nose sometimes changes with age and weather.

Jaws and Teeth—Strong, well set teeth, snugly overlapping with scissors bite. Undershot or overshot should be penalized.

(b) *Expression*—The expression, referred to as "Samoyed expression," is very important and is indicated by sparkle of the eyes, animation and lighting up of the face when alert or intent on anything. Expression is made up of a combination of

Ch. Suzanne of White Way, whelped in 1947. Bred by Agnes Mason and owned by Ed and Gertrude Adams.

American and Mexican Ch. Midnight Sun Kimba, owned by Kathi Horton and Art Mandale. Kimba was the 1972 Samoyed Club of America Specialty Best of Breed and has been among the top ten Samoyeds every year since.

eyes, ears and mouth. The ears should be erect when alert: the mouth should be slightly curved up at the corners to form the "Samoyed smile."

Torso—(a) *Neck*—Strong, well muscled, carried proudly erect, set on sloping shoulders to carry head with dignity when at attention. Neck should blend into shoulders with a graceful arch.

(b) *Chest*—Should be deep, with ribs well sprung out from the spine and flattened at the sides to allow proper movement of the shoulders and freedom for the front legs. Should not be barrel-chested. Perfect depth of chest approximates the point of elbows, and the deepest part of the chest should be back of the forelegs—near the ninth rib. Heart and lung room are secured more by body depth than width.

(c) *Loin and Back*—The withers forms the highest part of the back. Loins strong and slightly arched. The back should be straight to the loin, medium in length, very muscular and neither long nor short-coupled. The dog should be "just off square"—the length being approximately 5 per cent more than the height. Females allowed to be slightly longer than males. The belly should be well shaped and tightly muscled and, with the rear of the thorax, should swing up in a pleasing curve (tuck-up). Croup must be full, slightly sloping, and must continue imperceptibly to the tail root.

Tail—The tail should be moderately long with the tail bone terminating approximately at the hock when down. It should be profusely covered with long hair and carried forward over the back or side when alert, but sometimes dropped when at rest. It should not be high or low set and should be mobile and loose—not tight over the back. A double hook is a fault. A judge should see the tail over the back once when judging.

Disposition—Intelligent, gentle, loyal, adaptable, alert, full of action, eager to serve, friendly but conservative, not distrustful or shy, not overly aggressive. Unprovoked aggressiveness to be severely penalized.

DISQUALIFICATIONS

Any color other than pure white, cream, biscuit, or white and biscuit. Blue eyes.

Ch. Balalika's Roxanne of Forral, owned by Ed Altamirano and Bradley Forrest and bred by Walt and Jan Kauzlarich.

American and Canadian Ch. Kipperic Kandu of Suruka Orr, CD, top winning Samoyed bitch in 1972 and 1973. Owned by Don and Dot Hodges, Kandi was Best of Breed at the 1973 Samoyed Club of America Specialty.

The Samoyed Coat

The long, white, glistening coat is the first part of a Samoyed that catches the eye. Actually, a Samoyed has two coats: a long, coarse, stiff outer coat called a guard coat; and a shorter, fine, thick undercoat. The undercoat is a Samoyed's winter "long johns" and this is the coat that sheds in spring and fall.

Provided a Sammy gets regular weekly grooming, it is not difficult to keep him clean and shining. His skin and coat are not oily, so he has no strong, doggy smell, and the dirt does not stick to his harsh guard coat. *If* he has his weekly grooming, frequent baths are not necessary. But those twenty minute weekly grooming sessions are essential.

At the spring and fall shedding time, you will need to spend extra time, grooming your Samoyed daily, until all the loose hair has been combed out. A Sammy loses his coat almost all at once, so this seasonal shedding usually lasts about a week.

Grooming consists of brushing or combing the undercoat out from the skin, lifting it so it will support the guard coat and make both coats stand away from the body, giving the dog the characteristic fluffy, hairy look.

You will need a table for your Samoyed to lie or stand upon. Special rubber matted tables are available, or the top of his sleeping and traveling crate will provide a good place. (See illustration on page 36.)

Puppies should be groomed regularly. Puppy coat is soft, fine, and fuzzy, and you will need a soft nylon or natural-bristle brush (a woman's hair brush will do) so you will not pull and yank the coat. A pup likes to wiggle around and nibble on hands and brushes during grooming, so give your puppy a favorite toy to gnaw on. He should learn to be still and behave, and his first grooming sessions will deal with training as much as grooming.

When your puppy is between four and five months old, his coat will be ready for adult grooming tools. You will need a good pin brush with long metal bristles and a stiff, sturdy base; a slicker brush with small, short, bent metal bristles; a coarse toothed metal

American and Canadian Ch. Karatyll's Tia of Weathervane, owned and handled by John and Joan Scovin.

American, Mexican, and International Ch. Elrond Czar of Rivendell, CD, owned by Ed and Peggy Gaffney and bred by Burt and Mary Jo Kimbel.

comb; a fine toothed metal comb; toenail clippers; blunt nosed scissors; and thinning shears.

First, take the pin brush and brush vigorously opposite the direction of hair growth (from the tail toward the head). Brush the long hair, or feathering, on the rear of the back legs and hips downward; brush the tail from the base toward the tip.

Next, take the fine toothed comb and comb the hair on the forehead and ears, and the hair around the ears, using a gentle motion from the skin out to the tips of the hair. The hair just behind the ears is fine, wavy, and prone to matting. If a mat forms, do not cut it. Instead, work it loose with your fingers.

Now you are ready to groom the body. Take the slicker brush or the pin brush and, starting at the short hair on the back leg just above the joint, use your free hand to lift and part the hair and begin brushing straight out—from the skin to the hair tips. When one swath has been brushed, move your free hand up, releasing the next bit of ungroomed hair, and brush it straight out with a lifting movement. This brushing motion takes a little practice. It is a lifting and a fluffing and a brushing outward and a combing motion all at the same time, from the roots out. The touch should be gentle but purposeful.

When the thigh is brushed completely, move to the shoulder just even with the elbow and work up to the top of the shoulder. Then groom the side, starting low under the belly. Brush the chest between the front legs. When the first side is brushed, turn the dog and groom the thigh, shoulder, belly, and chest on the other side.

Next, start at the base of the tail and work toward the head, but brush toward the base of the tail. When you reach the long hair of the ruff, or mane, work facing the dog's head. Start between the ears and brush toward the nose, and move down the neck to the shoulders. Then start another swath behind an ear and work back to the shoulders. When brushing the sides of the neck, begin with the short hair around the face and work toward the shoulders, always brushing straight out and toward the face. For the neck under the muzzle, begin under the chin and brush up and out, working down to the chest. When grooming the ruff, keep in mind that you are brushing the undercoat up and out to support the long, heavy, harsh outer coat. When you are finished, the ruff should frame the face.

To groom the front legs, take the slicker brush and draw it straight up the leg. For the feathering on the back of the front legs, use the fine toothed comb, combing straight back and paying special attention to the elbows, where mats often develop.

On the back legs use the slicker brush to comb up the legs. The feathering on the back legs is short and fine, so use the fine toothed comb. The feathering on the back legs becomes ragged, so it will be necessary to trim these hairs to give a neat appearance. Use the thinning shears and carefully snip the hairs even. Do not clip close to the skin. The hairs should not look trimmed when you are finished: preserve the natural look.

The "trousers" are the long, thick feathering that grows on the back of the upper rear legs and hips. With the slicker brush or the pin brush, start just above the joint of the rear leg, using your free hand to part the coat, and brush-comb in a downward and outward direction. There is a spot just over the upper thigh where the coat gets flattened down because it is the contact point when the dog sits and lies down. This spot always needs extra attention.

Most dogs detest having the tail groomed, so do it last. Never, ever comb the tail. A comb pulls out the feathering on the tail, and it does not renew on a yearly basis as the rest of the coat does. Always use the pin brush, and work from the base to the tip. When finished, give the tail a gentle shake.

The final step is like the first. Take the pin brush and brush the entire coat vigorously toward the head. The hair over the hips where the tail lies when curled over the back should be smoothed by brushing it "flattish" toward the base of the tail. Brush the trousers outward and downward. When grooming is completed, a Samoyed always gives a little shake, and every hair in the coat puffs up—all fluffy, white, and lovely.

Now is the time for a treat, a small dog biscuit or a bite of kibble, so the dog will learn to associate grooming with a reward.

In grooming during the shedding period, the routine is the same. Use the coarse toothed comb or the slicker brush to pull the undercoat free, but take care not to yank and hurt the dog. The undercoat usually sheds twice a year: a heavy shedding in the spring, and a much lighter shedding in the fall. The guard coat does not renew each shedding, but when it does, it sheds out after the undercoat has begun to grow back in. If a dog's diet has been adequate, with plenty of high protein foods such as eggs and cottage cheese, the undercoat will grow in within six or eight weeks.

The average pet Samoyed will do very nicely with two or three baths a year if he is groomed regularly. If he leads a very active

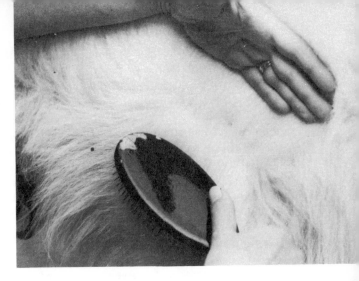

A Samoyed must be groomed from the skin out. Use the left hand to part and hold the hair not yet groomed, and with the pin brush in the right hand, brush the hair out from the skin and through the hair already brushed.

life, digging lots of holes, hiking and camping with his family, he will need bathing more frequently. A regular deep and careful grooming must always precede a bath. (For instructions on bathing the dog, see page 34.)

A forced hot air dryer is especially helpful in drying the coat of the Samoyed. Special dog hair dryers can be purchased, but a human hair dryer or a "hot comb" will do the job. You can skip this, but it will take forty-eight hours for an adult Sammy to air dry. It is important to keep the dog out of drafts if you do not use a dryer.

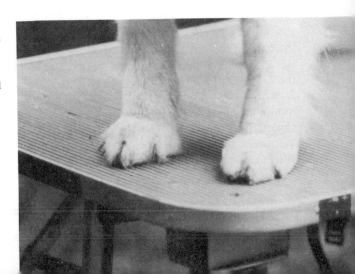

Hair on Samoyed's feet grows long both on bottom between pads and out from toes. It should be trimmed and evened with blunt-nosed scissors to prevent sore feet. Foot on left is untrimmed. Note how foot on right has been trimmed.

When you have finished bathing and rinsing the coat and have squeezed as much water as possible from the coat, rub the coat vigorously with towels to soak up more water. Then put a dry towel in the dog's crate or in another dry, clean place and let him lie on it and air dry for an hour or so while you clean up the bath equipment. Wash all brushes and combs after each bath.

After the dog has air dried for a time, place him on his grooming table and use the hair dryer to dry and fluff the coat, rubbing him with a dry towel as you go through the coat. Avoid blowing the air in his face. When he is almost dry, take the pin brush and use it to fluff and separate the hairs under the blower. Do not use the same combing motion you use during grooming. Use a very light, gentle, fluffing motion.

It takes two to four hours to dry a Samoyed under a blower, depending on the season of the year, the humidity, and the denseness of the coat. Always follow a bathing and drying session with a tidbit as a reward.

If you are preparing your dog for competition, it is best to bathe him two days before the show. Bathing softens the coat a little, but in a day or so the full harshness will return. Your Samoyed will need a thorough brushing and his whiskers should be trimmed before he goes in the ring.

Never, ever bathe a Sam while he is shedding! In the washing and rubbing, the coat will mat terribly. Always wait until the shedding is over and then bathe him.

The Samoyed has tough, hairy feet with strong, thick nails and thick pads which were developed on the tundra before the breed became "civilized." The nails grow rapidly and wear down slowly, and will need to be checked every two weeks to see if they need trimming. (See page 35 for instructions on trimming nails.)

The paws become very hairy between the pads and toes, and this hair, if not trimmed, will grow over the raspy pads and the dog will slip and fall on slick surfaces. Use the blunt nosed scissors to trim the hair on the bottoms of the feet even with the pads. Also, trim the long hairs which grow from the ends of the toes, and even up the hairs on the edges of the paws. Sometimes fine, fuzzy hairs grow up on the top of the feet. Trim these with short snips of the thinning shears, evening the hairs and shaping them over the paws. Hair on the feet usually needs to be trimmed only a couple of times a year. Since most dogs loathe having their feet handled, you may need help during foot grooming.

28

How to Make Use of All That Hair

There is a bonus for Samoyed owners at shedding time because the soft undercoat can be spun and then woven, knitted, or crocheted. People in the past have used dog hair for spinning. The Salish Indians of the North Pacific Coast had a long-haired white dog which they plucked. They mixed the hair with cedar bark fibers, spun it, and wove it into gorgeous, patterned blankets until the Hudson Bay blankets of the fur traders replaced their native handiworks. The Salish dog is now extinct, but a few of the blankets can still be seen in Canadian museums.

Samoyed hair is not easy to spin, but it makes a yarn that is light in weight and extremely warm. It does not wear well, however, so it is best suited for items that do not have to withstand heavy wear.

The undercoat from the sides and the neck of the dog is what is to be saved for spinning. The guard coat is coarse and scratchy and does not take a good twist. The hair from the legs is too short, and the hair from the back is too weathered. A lot of time can be saved if you sort the undercoat as you groom the dog. Discard any knots or debris, and, in sorting, remember—the shorter the fibers, the harder to spin. The suitable hair should be stored loosely in a paper bag so it can "breathe." It should never be shut up tightly or compacted. Hair that is not suitable for spinning can be used for stuffing throw pillows.

Before spinning, the hair must be carded. The cards are two steel bristled brushes which, as they are drawn across each other, align and prepare the hair into a small, loose roll called a "rolag." If you are a careful groomer, the undercoat will come off the grooming brush in a rolag and can be spun without carding.

Some spinners mix sheep wool with the dog hair to make a stronger yarn that is more easily spun. Carding the dog hair and wool together will mix it thoroughly. A sixty-percent Cheviot wool or comparable pure white medium staple wool should be used.

Equipment for spinning ranges from a primitive drop spindle to a modern electric spinner. There is a variety of foot propelled spinning wheels on the market, but avoid antique wheels, for they do not work as well as wheels of modern design.

Hair and wool are easier to work unwashed. Samoyed hair is difficult to spin because it is short and straight and does not take a twist easily. Experienced spinners recommend that the beginner

Spinning wheel, cards, and a spinning demonstration by Mrs. Carol Chittum, pictured here with Ch. Belaya Sarjeant Pepper, bred and owned by Mr. and Mrs. Chittum.

A "Ruana," a Colombian Indian shawl, made from Samoyed hair hand spun and woven by Mrs. Margo Gervolstad. The dog hair was collected from American and Canadian Ch. Zoder Ya Kut Blitz of Norgemar, CD, and American and Canadian Ch. Tsonqua of Snow Ridge, parents of the two-month-old puppy pictured with Mrs. Gervolstad.

learn to spin with sheep wool, and when he can make a good single ply wool yarn, then go to Samoyed hair. A single ply yarn is sufficient for any project using Samoyed hair.

Samoyed yarn can be worked in its natural color or it can be colored with commercial or vegetable dyes, for it takes dyes very well. Purists abhor commercial dyes, and, indeed, the subtle shading and earth tones of vegetable dyes cannot be equaled by aniline dyes.

Weaving equipment comes in as many different designs as spinning equipment. The most difficult part is preparing the loom with the warp threads so that the threads are evenly spaced and taut. The rest of the process is passing the weft thread through the warp and keeping it even. Pure Samoyed yarn must never be used for warp because it is not strong enough to hold the tension and take the stress of the shuttle, and it will break. For the warp, either a wool or a dog hair-wool mixture that is mostly wool should be used. For the weft, a yarn of dog hair and wool is best.

But the enjoyment of the Samoyed yarn does not depend upon expensive and complicated weaving equipment. The yarn can also be knitted or crocheted. One of the most beautiful Samoyed yarn projects the Author has ever seen is a knitted bedspread. The best use for pure Samoyed yarn is a knitted or crocheted scarf, stole, or tam in a loose, open pattern. For sweaters, it is best to use a yarn of dog hair mixed with wool, which gives added strength in such spots as elbows and necklines.

If you do not feel equal to the task of spinning the Samoyed hair into yarn, there are professional spinners who will do it for you. It takes two pounds of Samoyed undercoat to make a pound of finished yarn.

Ch. Sam O'Khan's Chingis Khan, owned by Jim and Joan Sheets. He was Samoyed Club of America's top winning Samoyed in years 1966 through 1970, and one of top ten dogs, all breeds, for 1967.

English import Suretta of Kobe with her six-week-old puppies sired by English Ch. Raff of Kobe. Suretta was imported by Billie Tucker in 1951.

Grooming the Family Dog

Every dog should be taught from puppyhood that a grooming session is a time for business, not for play. He should be handled gently, though, for it is essential to avoid hurting him in any way. Grooming time should be pleasant for both dog and master.

A light, airy, pleasant place in which to work is desirable, and it is of the utmost importance that neither dog nor master be distracted by other dogs, cats, or people. Consequently, it is usually preferable that grooming be done indoors.

Before each session, the dog should be permitted to relieve himself. Once grooming is begun, it is important to avoid keeping the dog standing so long that he becomes tired. If a good deal of grooming is needed, it should be done in two or more short periods.

A sturdy grooming table is desirable. The dog should stand on the grooming table while the back and upper portions of his body are groomed, and lie on his side while underparts of his body are brushed, nails clipped, etc.

It is almost impossible to brush too much, and show dogs are often brushed for a full half hour a day, year round. If you cannot brush your dog every day, you should brush him a minimum of two or three times a week. Brushing removes loose skin particles and stimulates circulation, thereby improving condition of the skin. It also stimulates secretion of the natural skin oils that make the coat look healthy and beautiful.

Before brushing, any burs adhering to the coat, as well as matted hair, should be carefully removed, using the fingers and coarse toothed comb with a gentle, teasing motion to avoid tearing the coat. The coat should first be brushed lightly in the direction in which the hair grows. Next, it should be brushed in the opposite direction, a small portion at a time, making sure the bristles penetrate the hair to the skin, until the entire coat has been brushed thoroughly and all loose soil removed. Then the coat should be brushed in the direction the hair grows, until every hair is sleekly in place.

The dog that is kept well brushed needs bathing only rarely. Once or twice a year is usually enough. If it is necessary to bathe a puppy, extreme care must be exercised so that he will not become chilled. No dog should be bathed during cold weather and then permitted to go outside immediately. Whatever the weather, the dog should always be given a good run outdoors and permitted to relieve himself before he is bathed.

Various types of "dry baths" are available, and in general, they are quite satisfactory when circumstances are such that a bath in water is impractical. Dry shampoos are usually worked into the dog's coat thoroughly, then removed by towelling or brushing.

Before starting a water bath, the necessary equipment should be assembled. This includes a tub of appropriate size, preferably one that has a drain so that the water will not accumulate and the dog will not be kept standing in water throughout the bath. A rubber mat should be placed in the bottom of the tub to prevent the dog from slipping. A small hose with a spray nozzle—one that may be attached to the water faucet—is ideal for wetting and rinsing the coat, but if such equipment is not available, then a second tub or a large pail should be provided for bath and rinse water. A metal or plastic cup for dipping water, special dog shampoo, a small bottle of mineral or olive oil, and a supply of absorbent cotton should be placed nearby, as well as a supply of heavy towels, a wash cloth, and the dog's combs and brushes. Bath water and rinse water should be slightly warmer than lukewarm, but should not be hot.

To avoid accidentally getting water in the dog's ears, place a small amount of absorbent cotton in each. With the dog standing in the tub, wet his body by using the hose and spray nozzle or by using the cup to pour water over him. Take care to avoid wetting the head, and be careful to avoid getting water or shampoo in the eyes. (If you should accidentally do so, placing a few drops of mineral or olive oil in the inner corner of the eye will bring relief.) When the dog is thoroughly wet, put a small amount of shampoo on his back and work the lather into the coat with a gentle, squeezing action. Wash the entire body and then use the cup and container of water (or hose and spray nozzle) to rinse the dog thoroughly.

Dip the wash cloth into clean water, wring it out enough so it won't drip, then wash the dog's head, taking care to avoid the eyes. Remove the cotton from the dog's ears and sponge them gently, inside and out. Shampoo should never be used inside the ears, so if they are extremely soiled, sponge them clean with cotton saturated with mineral or olive oil. (Between baths, the ears should be cleaned frequently in the same way.)

Quickly wrap a towel around the dog, remove him from the tub, and towel him as dry as possible. To avoid getting an impromptu bath yourself, you must act quickly, for once he is out of the tub, the dog will instinctively shake himself.

While the hair is still slightly damp, use a clean comb or brush to remove any tangles. If the hair is allowed to dry first, it may be completely impossible to remove them.

So far as routine grooming is concerned, the dog's eyes require little attention. Some dogs have a slight accumulation of mucus in the corner of the eyes upon waking mornings. A salt solution (a teaspoon of table salt to one pint of warm, sterile water) can be sponged around the eyes to remove the stain. During grooming sessions it is well to inspect the eyes, since many breeds are prone to eye injury. Eye problems of a minor nature may be treated at home (see page 54), but it is imperative that any serious eye abnormality be called to the attention of the veterinarian immediately.

Feeding hard dog biscuits and hard bones helps to keep tooth surfaces clean. Slight discoloration may be readily removed by rubbing with a damp cloth dipped in salt or baking soda. The dog's head should be held firmly, the lips pulled apart gently, and the teeth rubbed lightly with the dampened cloth. Regular care usually keeps the teeth in good condition, but if tartar accumulates, it should be removed by a veterinarian.

If the dog doesn't keep his nails worn down through regular exercise on hard surfaces, they must be trimmed at intervals, for nails that are too long may cause the foot to spread and thus spoil the dog's gait. Neglected nails may even grow so long that they will grow into a circle and puncture the dog's skin. Nails can be cut easily with any of the various types of nail trimmers. The cut is made just outside the faintly pink bloodline that can be seen on white nails. In pigmented nails, the bloodline is not easily seen, so the cut should be made just outside the hooklike projection on the underside of the nails. A few downward strokes with a nail file will smooth the cut surface, and, once shortened, nails can be kept short by filing at regular intervals.

Care must be taken that nails are not cut too short, since blood vessels may be accidentally severed. Should you accidentally cut a nail so short that it bleeds, apply a mild antiseptic and keep the dog quiet until bleeding stops. Usually, only a few drops of blood will be lost. But once a dog's nails have been cut painfully short, he will usually object when his feet are handled.

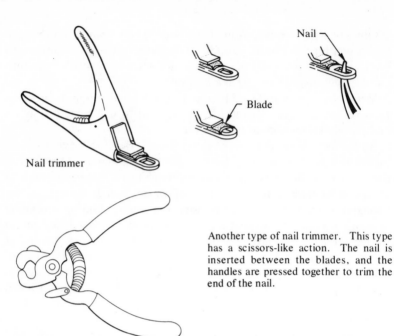

Nail trimmer

Blade

Nail

Another type of nail trimmer. This type has a scissors-like action. The nail is inserted between the blades, and the handles are pressed together to trim the end of the nail.

Dog crate with grooming-table top provides rigid, well supported surface on which to groom dog, and serves as indoor kennel for puppy or grown dog. Rubber matting provides non-slip surface. Dog's collar may be attached to adjustable arm.

Centered below is a grooming table with an adjustable arm to which the dog's collar may be attached. The adjustable arm at right below may be clamped to an ordinary table or other rigid surface which will serve as a grooming table.

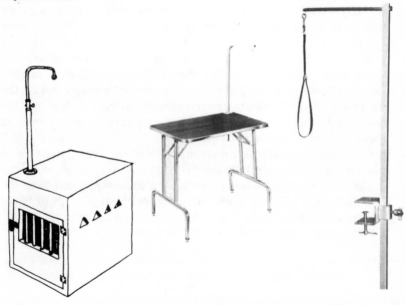

"Bed and Board" for the Family Dog

It is much easier to adapt to the demands of a new puppy if you collect the necessary equipment before you bring him home. You will need a water and food dish—preferably stainless steel and of a type that will not tip easily. You will need some chew toys, a soft puppy lead, and a soft hair brush for puppy grooming. You will need to decide where your dog is going to sleep and to prepare his bed.

Every dog should have a bed of his own, snug and warm, where he can retire undisturbed when he wishes to nap. And, especially with a small puppy, it is desirable to have the bed arranged so the dog can be securely confined at times, safe and contented. If the puppy is taught early in life to stay quietly in his box at night, or when the family is out, the habit will carry over into adulthood and will benefit both dog and master.

The dog should never be banished to a damp, cold basement, but should be quartered in an out-of-the-way corner close to the center of family activity. His bed can be an elaborate cushioned affair with electric warming pad, or simply a rectangular wooden box or heavy paper carton, cushioned with a clean cotton rug or towel. Actually, the latter is ideal for a new puppy, for it is snug, easy to clean, and expendable. A "door" can be cut on one side of the box for easy access, but it should be placed in such a way that the dog can still be confined when desirable.

The shipping crates used by professional handlers at dog shows make ideal indoor quarters. They are lightweight but strong, provide adequate air circulation, yet are snug and warm and easily cleaned. For the dog owner who takes his dog along when he travels, a dog crate is ideal, for the dog will willingly stay in his accustomed bed during long automobile trips, and the crate can be taken inside motels or hotels at night, making the dog a far more acceptable guest.

Dog crates are made of chromed metal or wood, and some have tops covered with a special rubber matting so they can be used as grooming tables. Anyone moderately handy with tools can construct a crate similar to the one illustrated on the opposite page.

Crates come in various sizes, to suit various breeds of dogs. For reasons of economy, the size selected for a puppy should be adequate for use when the dog is full grown. If the area seems too large when the puppy is small, a temporary cardboard partition can be installed to limit the area he occupies.

For the owner's convenience and to enhance the dog's sense of security, food and water dishes may be kept in the same general area where the crate is kept.

Nutrition

The main food elements required by dogs are proteins, fats, and carbohydrates. Vitamins A, B complex, D, and E are essential, as are ample amounts of calcium and iron. Nine other minerals are required in small amounts but are amply provided in almost any diet, so there is no need to be concerned about them.

The most important nutrient is protein and it must be provided every day of the dog's life, for it is essential for normal daily growth and replacement of body tissues burned up in daily activity. Preferred animal protein products are beef, mutton, horse meat, and boned fish. Visceral organs—heart, liver, and tripe—are good but if used in too large quantities may cause diarrhea (bones in large amounts have the same effect). Some veterinarians feel that pork is undesirable, while others consider lean pork acceptable as long as it is well cooked. Bacon drippings are often recommended for inclusion in the dog's diet, but this is a matter best discussed with your veterinarian since the salt in the bacon drippings might prove harmful to a dog that is not in good health. The "meat meal" used in some commercial foods is made from scrap meat processed at high temperatures and then dried. It is not quite so nutritious as fresh meat, but in combination with other protein products, it is an acceptable ingredient in the dog's diet.

Cooked eggs and raw egg yolk are good sources of protein, but raw egg white should never be fed since it may cause diarrhea. Cottage cheese and milk (fresh, dried, and canned) are high in protein, also. Puppies thrive on milk and it is usually included in the diet until the puppy is about three months of age, but when fed to older dogs it often causes diarrhea. Soy-bean meal, wheat germ meal, and dried brewers yeast are vegetable products high in protein and may be used to advantage in the dog's diet.

Vegetable and animal fats in moderate amounts should be used, especially if a main ingredient of the diet is dry or kibbled food. Fats should not be used excessively or the dog may become overweight.   Generally, fats should be increased slightly in the winter and reduced somewhat during warm weather.

Carbohydrates are required for proper assimilation of fats.   Dog biscuits, kibble, dog meal, and other dehydrated foods are good sources of carbohydrates, as are cereal products derived from rice, corn, wheat, and ground or rolled oats.

Vegetables supply additional proteins, vitamins, and minerals, and by providing bulk are of value in overcoming constipation. Raw or cooked carrots, celery, lettuce, beets, asparagus, tomatoes, and cooked spinach may be used.   They should always be chopped or ground well and mixed with the other food.   Various combinations may be used, but a good home-mixed ration for the mature dog consists of two parts of meat and one each of vegetables and dog meal (or cereal product).

Dicalcium phosphate and cod-liver oil are added to puppy diets to ensure inclusion of adequate amounts of calcium and Vitamins A and D.   Indiscriminate use of dietary supplements is not only unjustified but may be harmful and many breeders feel that their over-use may lead to excessive growth as well as to overweight at maturity.   Also, kidney damage in adult dogs has been traced to over-supplementation of the diet with calcium and Vitamin D.

Foods manufactured by well-known and reputable food processors are nutritionally sound and are offered in sufficient variety of flavors, textures, and consistencies that most dogs will find them tempting and satisfying.   Canned foods are usually "ready to eat," while dehydrated foods in the form of kibble, meal, or biscuits may require the addition of water or milk.   Dried foods containing fat sometimes become rancid, so to avoid an unpalatable change in flavor, the manufacturer may not include fat in dried food but recommend its addition at the time the water or milk is added.

Candy and other sweets are taboo, for the dog has no nutritional need for them and if he is permitted to eat them, he will usually eat less of foods he requires.   Also taboo are fried foods, highly seasoned foods, and extremely starchy foods, for the dog's digestive tract is not equipped to handle them.

Frozen foods should be thawed completely and warmed at least to lukewarm, while hot foods should be cooled to lukewarm.   Food should be in a fairly firm state, for sloppy food is difficult for the dog to digest.

Whether meat is raw or cooked makes little difference, so long as the dog is also given the juice that seeps from the meat during cooking. Bones provide little nourishment, although gnawing bones helps make the teeth strong and helps to keep tartar from accumulating on them. Beef bones, especially large knuckle bones, are best. Fish, poultry, and chop bones should never be given to dogs since they have a tendency to splinter and may puncture the dog's digestive tract.

Clean, fresh, cool water is essential and an adequate supply should be available twenty-four hours a day from the time the puppy is big enough to walk. Especially during hot weather, the drinking pan should be emptied and refilled at frequent intervals.

Puppies usually are weaned by the time they are six weeks old, so when you acquire a new puppy ten to twelve weeks old, he will already have been started on a feeding schedule. The breeder should supply exact details as to number of meals per day, types and amounts of food offered, etc. It is essential to adhere to this established routine, for drastic changes in diet may produce intestinal upsets. In most instances, a combination of dry meal, canned meat, and the plastic wrapped hamburger-like products provide a well-balanced diet. For a puppy that is too fat or too thin, or for one that has health problems, a veterinarian may recommend a specially formulated diet, but ordinarily, the commercially prepared foods can be used.

The amount of food offered at each meal must gradually be increased and by five months the puppy will require about twice what he needed at three months. However, the puppy should not be allowed to become too fat. Obesity has become a major health problem for dogs, and it is estimated that forty-one percent of American dogs are overweight. It is essential that weight be controlled throughout the dog's lifetime and that the dog be kept in trim condition—neither too fat nor too thin—for many physical problems can be traced directly to overweight. If the habit of overeating is developed in puppyhood, controlling the weight of the mature dog will be much more difficult.

A mature dog usually eats slightly less than he did as a growing puppy. For mature dogs, one large meal a day is usually sufficient, although some owners prefer to give two meals. As long as the dog enjoys optimum health and is neither too fat nor too thin, the number of meals a day makes little difference.

The amount of food required for mature dogs will vary. With canned dog food or home-prepared foods (that is, the combination of meat, vegetables, and meal), the approximate amount required is one-half ounce of food per pound of body weight. If the dog is fed a dehydrated commercial food, approximately one ounce of food is needed for each pound of body weight. Most manufacturers of commercial foods provide information on packages as to approximate daily needs of various breeds.

For most dogs, the amount of food provided should be increased slightly during the winter months and reduced somewhat during hot weather when the dog is less active.

As a dog becomes older and less active, he may become too fat. Or his appetite may decrease so he becomes too thin. It is necessary to adjust the diet in either case, for the dog will live longer and enjoy better health if he is maintained in trim condition. The simplest way to decrease or increase body weight is by decreasing or increasing the amount of fat in the diet. Protein content should be maintained at a high level throughout the dog's life.

If the older dog becomes reluctant to eat, it may be necessary to coax him with special food he normally relishes. Warming the food will increase its aroma and usually will help to entice the dog to eat. If he still refuses, rubbing some of the food on the dog's lips and gums may stimulate interest. It may be helpful also to offer food in smaller amounts and increase the number of meals per day. Foods that are highly nutritious and easily digested are especially desirable for older dogs. Small amounts of cooked, ground liver, cottage cheese, or mashed, hard-cooked eggs should be included in the diet often.

Before a bitch is bred, her owner should make sure that she is in optimum condition—slightly on the lean side rather than fat. The bitch in whelp is given much the same diet she was fed prior to breeding, with slight increases in amounts of meat, liver, and dairy products. Beginning about six weeks after breeding, she should be fed two meals per day rather than one, and the total daily intake increased. (Some bitches in whelp require as much as 50% more food than they consume normally.) She must not be permitted to become fat, for whelping problems are more likely to occur in overweight dogs. Cod-liver oil and dicalcium phosphate should be provided until after the puppies are weaned.

The dog used only occasionally for breeding will not require a special diet, but he should be well fed and maintained in optimum condition. A dog used frequently may require a slightly increased amount of food. But his basic diet will require no change so long as his general health is good and his flesh is firm and hard.

Dishes of this type are available in both plastic and stainless steel.

Crockery dish for food or water.

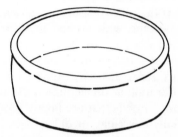

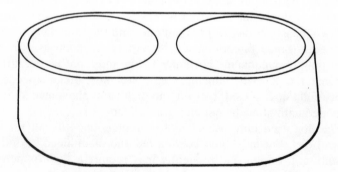

Stainless steel dish for food and water.

Maintaining the Dog's Health

In dealing with health problems, simple measures of preventive care are always preferable to cures—which may be complicated and costly. Many of the problems which afflict dogs can be avoided quite easily by instituting good dog-keeping practices in connection with feeding and housing.

Proper nutrition is essential in maintaining the dog's resistance to infectious diseases, in reducing susceptibility to organic diseases, and, of course, in preventing dietary deficiency diseases.

Cleanliness is essential in preventing the growth of disease-producing bacteria and other micro-organisms. All equipment, especially water and food dishes, must be kept immaculately clean. Cleanliness is also essential in controlling external parasites, which thrive in unsanitary surroundings.

Symptoms of Illness

Symptoms of illness may be so obvious there is no question that the dog is ill, or so subtle that the owner isn't sure whether there is a change from normal or not. **Loss of appetite, malaise** (general lack of interest in what is going on), **and vomiting** may be ignored if they occur singly and persist only for a day. However, in combination with other evidence of illness, such symptoms may be significant and the dog should be watched closely. **Abnormal bowel movements,** especially diarrhea or bloody stools, are causes for immediate concern. **Urinary abnormalities** may indicate infections, and bloody urine is always an indication of a serious condition. When a dog that has long been housebroken suddenly becomes incontinent, a veterinarian should be consulted, for he may be able to suggest treatment or medication that will be helpful.

Fever is a positive indication of illness and consistent deviation from the normal temperature range of 100 to 102 degrees is cause for concern. Have the dog in a standing position when taking his temperature. Coat the bulb of a rectal thermometer with petroleum jelly, raise the dog's tail, insert the thermometer to approximately half its length, and hold it in position for two minutes. Clean the thermometer with rubbing alcohol after each use and be sure to shake it down.

Fits, often considered a symptom of worms, may result from a variety of causes, including vitamin deficiencies, or playing to the point of exhaustion. A veterinarian should be consulted when a fit occurs, for it may be a symptom of serious illness.

Persistent coughing is often considered a symptom of worms, but may also indicate heart trouble—especially in older dogs.

Stary coat—dull and lackluster—indicates generally poor health and possible worm infestation. **Dull eyes** may result from similar conditions. Certain forms of blindness may also cause the eyes to lose the sparkle of vibrant good health.

Vomiting is another symptom often attributed to worm infestation. Dogs suffering from indigestion sometimes eat grass, apparently to induce vomiting and relieve discomfort.

Accidents and Injuries

Injuries of a serious nature—deep cuts, broken bones, severe burns, etc.—always require veterinary care. However, the dog may need first aid before being moved to a veterinary hospital.

A dog injured in any way should be approached cautiously, for reactions of a dog in pain are unpredictable and he may bite even a beloved master. A muzzle should always be applied before any attempt is made to move the dog or treat him in any way. The muzzle can be improvised from a strip of cloth, bandage, or even heavy cord, looped firmly around the dog's jaws and tied under the lower jaw. The ends should then be extended back of the neck and tied again so the loop around the jaws will stay in place.

A stretcher for moving a heavy dog can be improvised from a rug or board, and preferably two people should be available to transport it. A small dog can be carried by one person simply by grasping the loose skin at the nape of the neck with one hand and placing the other hand under the dog's hips.

Burns from chemicals should first be treated by flushing the coat with plain water, taking care to protect the dog's eyes and ears. A baking soda solution can then be applied to neutralize the chemical further. If the burned area is small, a bland ointment should be applied. If the burned area is large, more extensive treatment will be required, as well as veterinary care.

Burns from hot liquid or hot metals should be treated by applying a bland ointment, provided the burned area is small. Burns over large areas should be treated by a veterinarian.

Electric shock usually results because an owner negligently leaves an electric cord exposed where the dog can chew on it. If possible, disconnect the cord before touching the dog. Otherwise, yank the cord from the dog's mouth so you will not receive a shock when you try to help him. If the dog is unconscious, artificial respiration and stimulants will be required, so a veterinarian should be consulted at once.

Fractures require immediate professional attention. A broken bone should be immobilized while the dog is transported to the veterinarian but no attempt should be made to splint it.

Poisoning is more often accidental than deliberate, but whichever the case, symptoms and treatment are the same. If the poisoning is not discovered immediately, the dog may be found unconscious. His mouth will be slimy, he will tremble, have difficulty breathing, and possibly go into convulsions. Veterinary treatment must be secured immediately.

If you find the dog eating something you know to be poisonous, induce vomiting immediately by repeatedly forcing the dog to swallow a mixture of equal parts of hydrogen peroxide and water. Delay of even a few minutes may result in death. When the contents of the stomach have been emptied, force the dog to swallow raw egg white, which will slow absorption of the poison. Then call the veterinarian. Provide him with information as to the type of poison, and follow his advice as to further treatment.

Some chemicals are toxic even though not swallowed, so before using a product, make sure it can be used safely around pets.

Severe bleeding from a leg can be controlled by applying a tourniquet between the wound and the body, but the tourniquet must be loosened at ten-minute intervals. Severe bleeding from head or body can be controlled by placing a cloth or gauze pad over the wound, then applying firm pressure with the hand.

To treat minor cuts, first trim the hair from around the wound, then wash the area with warm soapy water and apply a mild antiseptic such as tincture of metaphen.

Shock is usually the aftermath of severe injury and requires immediate veterinary attention. The dog appears dazed, lips and tongue are pale, and breathing is shallow. The dog should be wrapped in blankets and kept warm, and if possible, kept lying down with his head lower than his body.

Bacterial and Viral Diseases

Distemper takes many and varied forms, so it is sometimes difficult for even experienced veterinarians to diagnose. It is the number one killer of dogs, and although it is not unknown in older dogs, its victims are usually puppies. While some dogs do recover, permanent damage to the brain or nervous system is often sustained. Symptoms may include lethargy, diarrhea, vomiting, reduced appetite, cough, nasal discharge, inflammation of the eyes, and a rise in temperature. If distemper is suspected, a veterinarian must be consulted at once, for early treatment is essential. Effective preventive measures lie in inoculation. Shots for temporary immunity should be given all puppies within a few weeks after whelping, and the permanent inoculations should be given as soon thereafter as possible.

Hardpad has been fairly prevalent in Great Britain for a number of years, and its incidence in the United States is increasing. Symptoms are similar to those of distemper, but as the disease progresses, the pads of the feet harden and eventually peel. Chances of recovery are not favorable unless prompt veterinary care is secured.

Infectious hepatitis in dogs affects the liver, as does the human form, but apparently is not transmissible to man. Symptoms are similar to those of distemper, and the disease rapidly reaches the acute state. Since hepatitis is often fatal, prompt veterinary treatment is essential. Effective vaccines are available and should be provided all puppies. A combination distemper-hepatitis vaccine is sometimes used.

Leptospirosis is caused by a micro-organism often transmitted by contact with rats, or by ingestion of food contaminated by rats. The disease can be transmitted to man, so anyone caring for an afflicted dog must take steps to avoid infection. Symptoms include vomiting, loss of appetite, diarrhea, fever, depression and lethargy, redness of eyes and gums, and sometimes jaundice. Since permanent kidney damage may result, veterinary treatment should be secured immediately.

Rabies is a disease that is always fatal—and it is transmissible to man. It is caused by a virus that attacks the nervous system and is present in the saliva of an infected animal. When an infected animal bites another, the virus is transmitted to the new victim. It may also enter the body through cuts and scratches that come in contact with saliva containing the virus.

All warm-blooded animals are subject to rabies and it may be transmitted by foxes, skunks, squirrels, horses, and cattle as well as dogs. Anyone bitten by a dog (or other animal) should see his physician immediately, and health and law enforcement officials should be notified. Also, if your dog is bitten by another animal, consult your veterinarian immediately.

In most areas, rabies shots are required by law. Even if not re-

46

quired, all dogs should be given anti-rabies vaccine, for it is an effective preventive measure.

Dietary Deficiency Diseases

Rickets afflicts puppies not provided sufficient calcium and Vitamin D. Symptoms include lameness, arching of neck and back, and a tendency of the legs to bow. Treatment consists of providing adequate amounts of dicalcium phosphate and Vitamin D and exposing the dog to sunlight. If detected and treated before reaching an advanced stage, bone damage may be lessened somewhat, although it cannot be corrected completely.

Osteomalacia, similar to rickets, may occur in adult dogs. Treatment is the same as for rickets, but here, too, prevention is preferable to cure. Permanent deformities resulting from rickets or osteomalacia will not be inherited, so once victims recover, they can be used for breeding.

External Parasites

Fleas, lice, mites, and ticks can be eradicated in the dog's quarters by regular use of one of the insecticide sprays with a four to six weeks' residual effect. Bedding, blankets, and pillows should be laundered frequently and treated with an insecticide. Treatment for external parasites varies, depending upon the parasite involved, but a number of good dips and powders are available.

Fleas may be eliminated by dusting the coat thoroughly with flea powder at frequent intervals during the summer months when fleas are a problem.

Flea collars are very effective in keeping a dog free of fleas. However, some animals are allergic to the chemicals in the collars, so caution must be observed when the collar is used and the skin of the neck area must be checked frequently and the collar removed if the skin becomes irritated. Care must also be taken that the collar is not fastened too tightly, and any excess at the end must be cut off to prevent the dog from chewing it. The collar should be removed if it becomes wet (or even damp) and should always be removed before the dog is bathed and not replaced around the dog's neck again until the coat is completely dry. For a dog which reacts to the flea collar, a medallion to be hung from the regular collar is available. This will eliminate direct skin contact and thus any allergic reaction will be avoided. The medallion should, of course, be removed when the dog is bathed.

Lice may be eradicated by applying dips formulated especially for this purpose to the dog's coat. A fine-toothed comb should

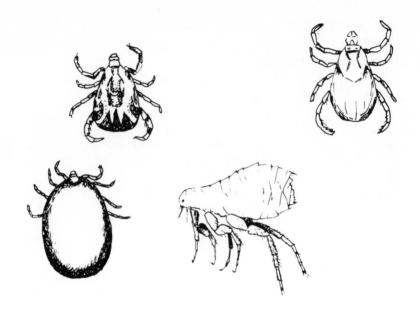

Common external parasites. Above, American dog ticks—left, female and right, male (much enlarged). Lower left, female tick, engorged. Lower right, dog flea (much enlarged).

then be used to remove dead lice and eggs, which are firmly attached to the coat.

Mites live deep in the ear canal, producing irritation to the lining of the ear and causing a brownish-black, dry type discharge. Plain mineral oil or ear ointment should be swabbed on the inner surface of the ear twice a week until mites are eliminated.

Ticks may carry Rocky Mountain spotted fever, so, to avoid possible infection, they should be removed from the dog only with tweezers and should be destroyed by burning (or by dropping them into insecticide). Heavy infestation can be controlled by sponging the coat daily with a solution containing a special tick dip.

Among other preparations available for controlling parasites on the dog's body are some that can be given internally. Since dosage must be carefully controlled, these preparations should not be used without consulting a veterinarian.

Internal Parasites

Internal parasites, with the exception of the tapeworm, may be transmitted from a mother dog to the puppies. Infestation may also result from contact with infected bedding or through access to a yard where an infected dog relieves himself. The types that may infest dogs are roundworms, whipworms, tapeworms, hookworms, and heartworms. All cause similar symptoms: a generally unthrifty appearance, stary coat, dull eyes, weakness and emaciation despite a ravenous appetite, coughing, vomiting, diarrhea, and sometimes bloody stools. Not all symptoms are present in every case, of course.

A heavy infestation with any type of worm is a serious matter and treatment must be started early and continued until the dog is free of the parasite or the dog's health will suffer seriously. Death may even result.

Promiscuous dosing for worms is dangerous and different types of worms require different treatment. So if you suspect your dog has worms, ask your veterinarian to make a microscopic examination of the feces, and to prescribe appropriate treatment if evidence of worm infestation is found.

LIFE CYCLE OF THE HEARTWORM

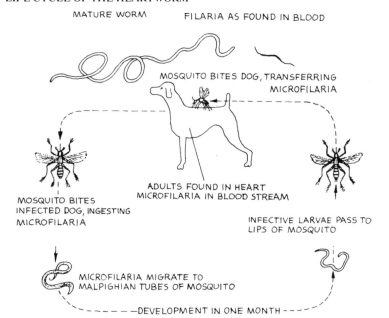

MATURE WORM   FILARIA AS FOUND IN BLOOD

MOSQUITO BITES DOG, TRANSFERRING MICROFILARIA

MOSQUITO BITES INFECTED DOG, INGESTING MICROFILARIA

ADULTS FOUND IN HEART
MICROFILARIA IN BLOOD STREAM

INFECTIVE LARVAE PASS TO LIPS OF MOSQUITO

MICROFILARIA MIGRATE TO MALPIGHIAN TUBES OF MOSQUITO

- - - - DEVELOPMENT IN ONE MONTH - - - -

Heartworms were once thought to be a problem confined to the Southern part of the United States but they have become an increasingly common problem in Middle Western States. The larva is transmitted from dog to dog through the bite of the mosquito, and eight to nine months may elapse from the time the dog is bitten until the heartworm is mature. Once they have entered the bloodstream, heartworms mature in the heart, where they interfere with heart action. Symptoms include lethargy, chronic coughing, and loss of weight. Having the dog's blood examined microscopically is the only way the tiny larvae (called microfilaria) can be detected. Eradication of heartworms is extremely difficult, so a veterinarian well versed in this field should be consulted. In an area where mosquitoes are prevalent, it is well to protect the dog by keeping him in a screened-in area.

Hookworms are found in puppies as well as adult dogs. When excreted in the feces, the mature worm looks like a thread and is about three-quarters of an inch in length. Eradication is a serious problem in areas where the soil is infested with the worms, for the dog may then become reinfested after treatment. Consequently, medication usually must be repeated at intervals, and the premises—including the grounds where the dog exercises—must be treated and must be kept well drained. You may wish to consult your veterinarian regarding the vaccine for the prevention of hookworms in dogs which was licensed recently by the United States Department of Agriculture.

Roundworms are the most common of all the worms that may infest the dog, for most puppies are born with them or become infested with them shortly after birth. Roundworms vary in length from two to eight inches and can be detected readily through microscopic examination of the feces. At maturity, upon excretion, the roundworm will spiral into a circle, but after it dies it resembles a cut rubber band.

If you suspect that a puppy may have roundworms, check its gums and tongue. If the puppy is heavily infested, the worms will cause anemia and the gums and the tongue will be a very pale pink color. If the puppy is anemic, the veterinarian probably will prescribe a tonic in addition to the proper worm medicine.

Tapeworms require an intermediate host, usually the flea or the louse, but they sometimes are found in raw fish, so a dog can become infested by swallowing a flea or a louse, or by eating infested fish.

LIFE CYCLE OF THE HOOKWORM

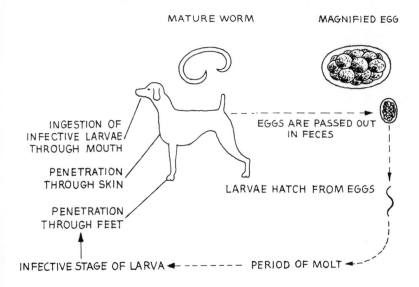

MATURE WORM   MAGNIFIED EGG

INGESTION OF
INFECTIVE LARVAE
THROUGH MOUTH

PENETRATION
THROUGH SKIN

PENETRATION
THROUGH FEET

EGGS ARE PASSED OUT
IN FECES

LARVAE HATCH FROM EGGS

INFECTIVE STAGE OF LARVA ← - - - - - - PERIOD OF MOLT ←- -

LIFE CYCLE OF THE COMMON ROUNDWORM

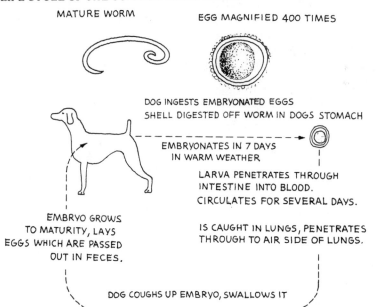

MATURE WORM   EGG MAGNIFIED 400 TIMES

DOG INGESTS EMBRYONATED EGGS
SHELL DIGESTED OFF WORM IN DOGS STOMACH

EMBRYONATES IN 7 DAYS
IN WARM WEATHER

LARVA PENETRATES THROUGH
INTESTINE INTO BLOOD.
CIRCULATES FOR SEVERAL DAYS.

EMBRYO GROWS
TO MATURITY, LAYS
EGGS WHICH ARE PASSED
OUT IN FECES.

IS CAUGHT IN LUNGS, PENETRATES
THROUGH TO AIR SIDE OF LUNGS.

DOG COUGHS UP EMBRYO, SWALLOWS IT

LIFE CYCLE OF THE FLEA-HOST TAPEWORM
MATURE WORM ———— CAPSULE WITH EGGS

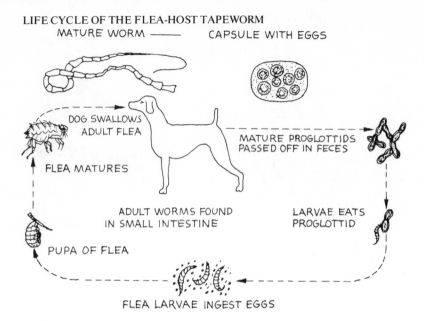

A complete tapeworm can be two to three feet long. The head and neck of the tapeworm are small and threadlike, while the body is made up of segments like links of a sausage, which are about half an inch long and flat. Segments of the body separate from the worm and will be found in the feces or will hang from the coat around the anus and when dry will resemble dark grains of rice.

The head of the tapeworm is imbedded in the lining of the intestine where the worm feeds on the blood of the dog. The difficulty

LIFE CYCLE OF THE WHIPWORM
MATURE WORM   MAGNIFIED EGG

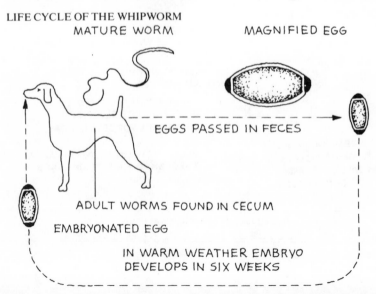

in eradicating the tapeworm lies in the fact that most medicines have a laxative action which is too severe and which pulls the body from the head so the body is eliminated with the feces, but the implanted head remains to start growing a new body. An effective medication is a tablet which does not dissolve until it reaches the intestine where it anesthetizes the worm to loosen the head before expulsion.

Whipworms are more common in the eastern states than in states along the West Coast, but whipworms may infest dogs in any section of the United States. Whipworms vary in length from two to four inches and are tapered in shape so they resemble a buggy whip—which accounts for the name.

At maturity, the whipworm migrates into the caecum, where it is difficult to reach with medication. A fecal examination will show whether whipworms are present, so after treatment, it is best to have several examinations made in order to be sure the dog is free of them.

Skin Problems

Skin problems usually cause persistent itching. However, **follicular mange** does not usually do so but is evidenced by moth-eaten-looking patches, especially about the head and along the back. **Sarcoptic mange** produces severe itching and is evidenced by patchy, crusty areas on body, legs, and abdomen. Any evidence suggesting either should be called to the attention of a veterinarian. Both require extensive treatment and both may be contracted by humans.

Allergies are not readily distinguished from other skin troubles except through laboratory tests. However, dog owners should be alert to the fact that various coat dressings and shampoos, or simply bathing the dog too often, may produce allergic skin reactions.

Eczema is characterized by extreme itching, redness of the skin and exudation of serous matter. It may result from a variety of causes, and the exact cause in a particular case may be difficult to determine. Relief may be secured by dusting the dog twice a week with a soothing powder containing a fungicide and an insecticide.

Other Health Problems

Clogged anal glands cause intense discomfort, which the dog may attempt to relieve by scooting himself along the floor on his haunches. These glands, located on either side of the anus, se-

crete a substance that enables the dog to expel the contents of the rectum. If they become clogged, they may give the dog an unpleasant odor and when neglected, serious infection may result. Contents of the glands can be easily expelled into a wad of cotton, which should be held under the tail with the left hand. Then, using the right hand, pressure should be exerted with the thumb on one side of the anus, the forefinger on the other. The normal secretion is brownish in color, with an unpleasant odor. The presence of blood or pus indicates infection and should be called to the attention of a veterinarian.

Eye problems of a minor nature—redness or occasional discharge—may be treated with a few drops of boric acid solution (2%) or salt solution (1 teaspoonful table salt to 1 pint sterile water). Cuts on the eyeball, bruises close to the eyes, or persistent discharge should be treated only by a veterinarian.

Heat exhaustion is a serious (and often fatal) problem caused by exposure to extreme heat. Usually it occurs when a thoughtless owner leaves the dog in a closed vehicle without proper shade and ventilation. Even on a day when outside temperatures do not seem excessively high, heat builds up rapidly to an extremely high temperature in a closed vehicle parked in direct sunlight or even in partial shade. Many dogs and young children die each year from being left in an inadequately ventilated vehicle. To prevent such a tragedy, an owner or parent should never leave a dog or child unattended in a vehicle even for a short time.

During hot weather, whenever a dog is taken for a ride in an air-conditioned automobile, the cool air should be reduced gradually when nearing the destination, for the sudden shock of going from cool air to extremely hot temperatures can also result in shock and heat exhaustion.

Symptoms of heat exhaustion include rapid and difficult breathing and near or complete collapse. After removing the victim from the vehicle, first aid treatment consists of sponging cool water over the body to reduce temperature as quickly as possible. Immediate medical treatment is essential in severe cases of heat exhaustion.

Care of the Ailing or Injured Dog

A dog that is seriously ill, requiring surgical treatment, transfusions, or intravenous feeding, must be hospitalized. One requiring less complicated treatment is better cared for at home, but it is essential that the dog be kept in a quiet environment. Preferably his bed should be in a room apart from family activity, yet close at hand, so his condition can be checked frequently. Clean bedding and adequate warmth are essential, as are a constant supply of fresh, cool water, and foods to tempt the appetite.

Special equipment is not ordinarily needed, but the following items will be useful in caring for a sick dog, as well as in giving first aid for injuries:

petroleum jelly	tincture of metaphen
rubbing alcohol	cotton, gauze, and adhesive tape
mineral oil	burn ointment
rectal thermometer	tweezers
hydrogen peroxide	boric acid solution (2%)

If special medication is prescribed, it may be administered in any one of several ways. A pill or small capsule may be concealed in a small piece of meat, which the dog will usually swallow with no problem. A large capsule may be given by holding the dog's mouth open, inserting the capsule as far as possible down the throat, then holding the mouth closed until the dog swallows. Liquid medicine should be measured into a small bottle or test tube. Then, if the corner of the dog's lip is pulled out while the head is tilted upward, the liquid can be poured between the lips and teeth, a small amount at a time. If he refuses to swallow, keeping the dog's head tilted and stroking his throat will usually induce swallowing.

Liquid medication may also be given by use of a hypodermic syringe without a needle. The syringe is slipped into the side of the mouth and over the rise at the back of the tongue, and the medicine is "injected" slowly down the throat. This is especially good for medicine with a bad taste, for the medicine does not touch the taste buds in the front part of the tongue. It also eliminates spills and guarantees that all the medicine goes in.

Foods offered the sick dog should be particularly nutritious and easily digested. Meals should be smaller than usual and offered at more frequent intervals. If the dog is reluctant to eat, offer food he particularly likes and warm it slightly to increase aroma and thus make it more tempting.

The Stone-Age Dog.

A Spotted Dog from India, "Parent of the modern Coach Dog."

History of the Genus Canis

The history of man's association with the dog is a fascinating one, extending into the past at least seventy centuries, and involving the entire history of civilized man from the early Stone Age to the present.

The dog, technically a member of the genus *Canis,* belongs to the zoological family group *Canidae,* which also includes such animals as wolves, foxes, jackals, and coyotes. In the past it was generally agreed that the dog resulted from the crossing of various members of the family *Canidae.* Recent findings have amended this theory somewhat, and most authorities now feel the jackal probably has no direct relationship with the dog. Some believe dogs are descended from wolves and foxes, with the wolf the main progenitor. As evidence, they cite the fact that the teeth of the wolf are identical in every detail with those of the dog, whereas the teeth of the jackal are totally different.

Still other authorities insist that the dog always has existed as a separate and distinct animal. This group admits that it is possible for a dog to mate with a fox, coyote, or wolf, but points out that the resulting puppies are unable to breed with each other, although they can breed with stock of the same genus as either parent. Therefore, they insist, it was impossible for a new and distinct genus to have developed from such crossings. They then cite the fact that any dog can be mated with any other dog and the progeny bred among themselves. These researchers point out, too, heritable characteristics that are different in these animals. For instance, the pupil of the eye of the fox is eliptical and vertical, while the pupil is round in the dog, wolf, and coyote. Tails, too, differ considerably, for tails of foxes, coyotes, and wolves always drop behind them, while those of dogs may be carried over the back or straight up.

Much conjecture centers on two wild dog species that still exist—the Dingo of Australia, and the Dhole in India. Similar in appearance, both are reddish in color, both have rather long, slender jaws, both have rounded ears that stand straight up, and both species hunt in packs. Evidence indicates that they had the same ancestors. Yet, today, they live in areas that are more than 4,000 miles apart.

Despite the fact that it is impossible to determine just when the dog first appeared as a distinct species, archeologists have found definite proof that the dog was the first animal domesticated by man. When man lived by tracking, trapping, and killing game, the dog added to the forces through which man discovered and captured the quarry. Man shared his primitive living quarters with the dog, and the two together devoured the prey. Thus, each helped to sustain the life of the other. The dog assisted man, too, by defending the campsite against marauders. As man gradually became civilized, the dog's usefulness was extended to guarding the other animals man domesticated, and, even before the wheel was invented, the dog served as a beast of burden. In fact, archeological findings show that aboriginal peoples of Switzerland and Ireland used the dog for such purposes long before they learned to till the soil.

Cave drawings from the palaeolithic era, which was the earliest part of the Old World Stone Age, include hunting scenes in which a rough, canine-like form is shown alongside huntsmen. One of these drawings is believed to be 50,000 years old, and gives credence to the theory that all dogs are descended from a primitive type ancestor that was neither fox nor wolf.

Archeological findings show that Europeans of the New Stone Age possessed a breed of dogs of wolf-like appearance, and a similar breed has been traced through the successive Bronze Age and Iron Age. Accurate details are not available, though, as to the external appearance of domesticated dogs prior to historic times (roughly four to five thousand years ago).

Early records in Chaldean and Egyptian tombs show that several distinct and well-established dog types had been developed by about 3700 B.C. Similar records show that the early people of the Nile Valley regarded the dog as a god, often burying it as a mummy in special cemeteries and mourning its death.

Some of the early Egyptian dogs had been given names, such as Akna, Tarn, and Abu, and slender dogs of the Greyhound type and a short-legged Terrier type are depicted in drawings found in Egyptian royal tombs that are at least 5,000 years old. The Afghan Hound and the Saluki are shown in drawings of only slightly later times. Another type of ancient Egyptian dog was much heavier and more powerful, with short coat and massive head. These

Bas-relief of Hunters with Nets and Mastiffs. From the walls of Assurbanipal's palace at Nineveh 668-626 B.C. *British Museum.*

probably hunted by scent, as did still another type of Egyptian dog that had a thick furry coat, a tail curled almost flat over the back, and erect "prick" ears.

Early Romans and Greeks mentioned their dogs often in literature, and both made distinctions between those that hunted by sight and those that hunted by scent. The Romans' canine classifications were similar to those we use now. In addition to dogs comparable to the Greek sight and scent hounds, the ancient Romans had Canes *villatici* (housedogs) and Canes *pastorales* (sheepdogs), corresponding to our present-day working dogs.

The dog is mentioned many times in the Old Testament. The first reference, in Genesis, leads some Biblical scholars to assert that man and dog have been companions from the time man was created. And later Biblical references bring an awareness of the diversity in breeds and types existing thousands of years ago.

As civilization advanced, man found new uses for dogs. Some required great size and strength. Others needed less of these characteristics but greater agility and better sight. Still others

59

needed an accentuated sense of smell. As time went on, men kept those puppies that suited specific purposes especially well and bred them together. Through ensuing generations of selective breeding, desirable characteristics appeared with increasing frequency. Dogs used in a particular region for a special purpose gradually became more like each other, yet less like dogs of other areas used for different purposes. Thus were established the foundations for the various breeds we have today.

The American Kennel Club, the leading dog organization in the United States, divides the various breeds into six "Groups," based on similarity of purposes for which they were developed.

"Sporting Dogs" include the Pointers, Setters, Spaniels, and Retrievers that were developed by sportsmen interested in hunting game birds. Most of the Pointers and Setters are of comparatively recent origin. Their development parallels the development of sporting firearms, and most of them evolved in the British Isles. Exceptions are the Weimaraner, which was developed in Germany, and the Vizsla, or Hungarian Pointer, believed to have been developed by the Magyar hordes that swarmed over Central Europe a

Bas-relief of Assyrian Mastiffs hunting wild horses. *British Museum.*

thousand years ago. The Irish were among the first to use Spaniels, though the name indicates that the original stock may have come from Spain. Two Sporting breeds, the American Water Spaniel and the Chesapeake Bay Retriever, were developed entirely in the United States.

"Hounds," among which are Dachshunds, Beagles, Bassets, Harriers, and Foxhounds, are used singly, in pairs, or in packs to "course" (or run) and hunt for rabbits, foxes, and various rodents. But little larger, the Norwegian Elkhound is used in its native country to hunt big game—moose, bear, and deer.

The smaller Hound breeds hunt by scent, while the Irish Wolfhound, Borzoi, Scottish Deerhound, Saluki, and Greyhound hunt by sight. The Whippet, Saluki, and Greyhound are notably fleet of foot, and racing these breeds (particularly the Greyhound) is popular sport.

The Bloodhound is a member of the Hound Group that is known world-wide for its scenting ability. On the other hand, the Basenji is a comparatively rare Hound breed and has the distinction of being the only dog that cannot bark.

"Working Dogs" have the greatest utilitarian value of all modern dogs and contribute to man's welfare in diverse ways. The Boxer, Doberman Pinscher, Rottweiler, German Shepherd, Great Dane, and Giant Schnauzer are often trained to serve as sentries and aid police in patrolling streets. The German Shepherd is especially noted as a guide dog for the blind. The Collie, the various breeds of Sheepdogs, and the two Corgi breeds are known throughout the world for their extraordinary herding ability. And the exploits of the St. Bernard and Newfoundland are legendary, their records for saving lives unsurpassed.

The Siberian Husky, the Samoyed, and the Alaskan Malamute are noted for tremendous strength and stamina. Had it not been for these hardy Northern breeds, the great polar expeditions might never have taken place, for Admiral Byrd used these dogs to reach points inaccessible by other means. Even today, with our jet-age transportation, the Northern breeds provide a more practical means of travel in frigid areas than do modern machines.

"Terriers" derive their name from the Latin *terra*, meaning "earth," for all of the breeds in this Group are fond of burrowing. Terriers hunt by digging into the earth to rout rodents and fur-bearing animals such as badgers, woodchucks, and otters. Some breeds are expected merely to force the animals from their dens in

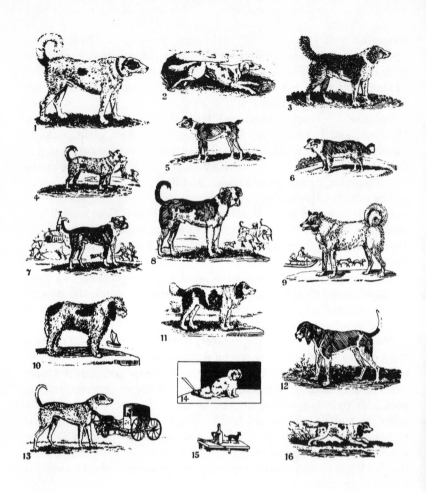

1. The Newfoundland. 2. The English Setter. 3. The Large Water-spaniel. 4. The Terrier. 5. The Cur-dog. 6. The Shepherd's Dog. 7. The Bulldog. 8. The Mastiff. 9. The Greenland Dog. 10. The Rough Water-dog. 11. The Small Water-spaniel. 12. The Old English Hound. 13. The Dalmatian or Coach-dog. 14. The Comporter (very much of a Papillon). 15. "Toy Dog, Bottle, Glass, and Pipe." *From a vignette.* 16. The Springer or Cocker. *From Thomas Bewick's "General History of Quadrupeds" (1790).*

order that the hunter can complete the capture. Others are expected to find and destroy the prey, either on the surface or under the ground.

Terriers come in a wide variety of sizes, ranging from such large breeds as the Airedale and Kerry Blue to such small ones as the Skye, the Dandie Dinmont, the West Highland White, and the Scottish Terrier. England, Ireland, and Scotland produced most of the Terrier breeds, although the Miniature Schnauzer was developed in Germany.

"Toys," as the term indicates, are small breeds. Although they make little claim to usefulness other than as ideal housepets, Toy dogs develop as much protective instinct as do larger breeds and serve effectively in warning of the approach of strangers.

Origins of the Toys are varied. The Pekingese was developed as the royal dog of China more than two thousand years before the birth of Christ. The Chihuahua, smallest of the Toys, originated in Mexico and is believed to be a descendant of the Techichi, a dog of great religious significance to the Aztecs, while the Italian Greyhound was popular in the days of ancient Pompeii.

"Non-Sporting Dogs" include a number of popular breeds of varying ancestry. The Standard and Miniature Poodles were developed in France for the purpose of retrieving game from water. The Bulldog originated in Great Britain and was bred for the purpose of "baiting" bulls. The Chow Chow apparently originated centuries ago in China, for it is pictured in a bas relief dated to the Han dynasty of about 150 B.C.

The Dalmatian served as a carriage dog in Dalmatia, protecting travelers in bandit-infested regions. The Keeshond, recognized as the national dog of Holland, is believed to have originated in the Arctic or possibly the Sub-Arctic. The Schipperke, sometimes erroneously described as a Dutch dog, originated in the Flemish provinces of Belgium. And the Lhasa Apso came from Tibet, where it is known as "Abso Seng Kye," the "Bark Lion Sentinel Dog."

During the thousands of years that man and dog have been closely associated, a strong affinity has been built up between the two. The dog has more than earned his way as a helper, and his faithful, selfless devotion to man is legendary. The ways in which the dog has proved his intelligence, his courage, and his dependability in situations of stress are amply recorded in the countless tales of canine heroism that highlight the pages of history, both past and present.

Dogs in Woodcuts. (*1st row*) (LEFT) "Maltese dog with shorter hair"; (RIGHT) "Spotted sporting dog trained to catch game"; (*2nd row*) (LEFT) Sporting white dog; (RIGHT) "Spanish dog with floppy ears": (*3rd row*) (LEFT) "French dog"; (RIGHT) "Mad dog of Grevinus"; (*4th row*) (LEFT) Hairy Maltese dog; (RIGHT) "English fighting dog . . . of horrid aspect." *From Aldrovandus (1637).*

History of the Samoyed

The Samoyed is a natural breed. That is, the early breeding stock was collected from native haunts among the Samoyede tribes rather than being created by crossbreeding and selection. The Samoyed was modified only slightly by the dog fanciers of Edwardian England to whom the ownership of a new or rare breed of dogs was a status symbol.

The Samoyed dog is the product of the Samoyede people who, in Czarist Russia, occupied the tundra region from the Khatanga River of North Central Siberia to the Kola Peninsula in Northern Europe. The Samoyedes are an extremely ancient people, Mongoloid in racial stock, Ural-Altaic in linguistic stock, and Magdalenian in cultural descent, which makes them cultural cousins of the Paleo-Siberian tribes and the North American Eskimos.

Today in the U.S.S.R., the Samoyedes are called "the Nentsi" and live on collective farms in the vicinity of the Yamal Peninsula. Their dogs are much mongrellized, being small and mostly red and white spotted in color.

The Samoyedes and their neighbors in the old days referred to the Samoyedes' dogs as "Bjelkiers," best translated as "the Whities," although many individuals were light red-brown, or spotted white and red-brown, or spotted white and black. The Whities were considered a distinct breed from dogs of the Ostyaks and the Yakuts. The "Whities" were house dogs and were reported to be much more gentle, friendly, and desirous of human associations, and to be superb and fearless hunters, particularly of bears.

The first European to use the Samoyed dog and record his adventures in detail was the Norwegian explorer, Fridtjof Nansen. His dogs were purchased by Alexander Trontheim in the vicinity of the Ob River in 1894. Nansen's plan was to freeze his ship the "Fram" into the ice of the Arctic Ocean and drift with the ice across the North Pole. When it became clear they were drifting too far south, Nansen and his associate, Johannsen, set out with dog teams and sledges for the Pole. They did not reach it, but they did eventually reach safety. The dogs did not; they were fed to

Young Samoyeds by Peter the Great out of Alaska, bred by The Honorable Mrs. McLaren Morrison. (From *The New Book of the Dog,* by Robert Leighton, 1911.)

Ch. "Antarctic Bru," the property of Mrs. Kilburn Scott. (From *Dogs, Their History and Development*, by Robert C. Ash.)

Pictured here are the bear hunting dogs used on the Jackson-Harmsworth expedition to Franz Joseph Land. On the left is Major Frederick Jackson with Sally, Nimrod, and Räwing. On the right is A. B. Armitage with Sammie.

each other when supplies ran low, and finally, the two surviving dogs, Suggen and Kaifas, were shot because Nansen and Johannsen had reached open water and would be spending several weeks at sea in kayaks. Later, Nansen had praise for the Samoyed dog and some regrets.

The next expedition to the Arctic, the Jackson-Harmsworth group, went to Franz Joseph Land in 1894 to map the area and gather data on the climate. The dogs for the expedition were acquired on the mainland, and Jackson's favorites were Sally, Nimrod, and Räwing. They were his bear hunting dogs. Sally and Nimrod could step into the show ring today, and Räwing was a typical Samoyed except that he was black and white. When the work of the expedition was completed, all of the surviving dogs were shipped home to England.

The Italian expedition of the Duc d'Abruzzi also aspired to reach the North Pole, and upon the advice of Nansen used Samoyed dogs and had Trontheim acquire them in Siberia in 1898.

Carsten Borchgrevink, a Norwegian, led an English expedition to the Antarctic in 1898 and used Samoyeds acquired in Siberia by a trader named Siberiakoff. After the expedition returned to New Zealand, the dogs were kenneled there on Stewart Island.

Sir Ernest Shackleton, on his 1907-1909 expedition to the Antarctic, used the white dogs from Stewart Island, although he preferred ponies. In later expeditions, he gave up ponies and used dogs exclusively.

Captain Robert Scott, on his 1901-1903 expedition, took Samoyed dogs with him that had been collected by Trontheim in Siberia. But in his dash to the South Pole in the winter of 1911-1912, he used ponies.

The first to reach the South Pole was Roald Amundsen, who arrived there December 14, 1911. He used mixed teams of Greenland Eskimo dogs and Samoyeds; and his success with dog teams was the result of his care in selecting the dogs and the pains he took in training them. He, also, ended up feeding the weaker to the stronger dogs to make it back from the Pole. Some of his surviving dogs went with another expedition, but most went home with expedition members and crew as pets.

All these expedition dogs are of the utmost importance, because from them came the foundation stock for today's Samoyed dog.

The first Samoyed to become an ancestor of the modern breed was Sabarka. Ernest Kilburn-Scott acquired him as a puppy in

Archangel in 1889 as a gift for his wife. Sabarka was a deep brown with white paws and a white patch on his chest. The Kilburn-Scotts were the leaders among early Samoyed breeders in England and were responsible for the breed's being named "Samoyed." Some had wanted to use the name Nordic Spitz, but the Kilburn-Scotts prevailed and in 1892 the name Samoyede, after the tribe, became official. Later, the final "e" was dropped.

Shortly after Sabarka came to England, the Kilburn-Scotts imported a cream colored bitch, Whitey Petchora, which they bred to Sabarka. Among the puppies were Peter the Great and Neva.

Neva was purchased by Lady Sitwell, who later imported Musti, a white male, from Siberia. Musti was also bred to Whitey Petchora and produced Nansen, a white who was shown but never made his championship. Nansen was the sire of several early champions.

In 1899 Frederick Jackson returned from Franz Joseph Land with his expedition dogs. Besides his bear dog, Nimrod, seven other dogs went to the Kilburn-Scotts. They were Kvik, Flo, Yugor, Jenny, Mamax, and Gladys. The bitches Kvik and Flo were of the greatest influence. Jacko, a half brother of Flo and a son of Nimrod, was given by Jackson to Queen Alexandra, who had several Samoyeds at the kennels at Sandringham. Her dogs were shown regularly.

When Trontheim acquired the dogs for the Duc d'Abruzzi expedition in 1894, he also selected a white male for the Kilburn-Scotts. Russ was bred to the expedition bitch Kvik in 1901 and produced the second champion and first champion bitch, Ch. Pearlene, who was a white with excellent conformation and good black points. Russ was also bred to the expedition bitch Flo and produced the third champion, also a bitch, Ch. Alaska, owned by Mrs. MacLaren Morrison.

In 1908 the Kilburn-Scotts brought Antarctic Buck to England. He was a descendant of the dogs on the Borchgrevink Expedition and had been on display in the Sydney Zoo. In England he was bred to Kviklene, a daughter of Nansen and Ch. Pearlene, to produce an all male litter of Ch. Fang, South Pole, Southern Cross, Olaf, and Mezenit. Bred to Olgalene, a daughter of Musti and Whitey Petchora, Antarctic Buck produced Ch. Kaifas and Ch. Kirche. Antarctic Buck was notable for his excellent conformation and substance, and, most of all, for his glistening white coat, which he passed on to his progeny. His sons were much bred from and continued to throw his best qualities. Olaf was a member of Scott's last expedition but was left behind in New Zealand as a pet.

Another dog, Trip, also descended from Borchgrevink's dogs, went on Shackelton's expedition in 1911. He went to England with Lieutenant Adams and was given to Mrs. Kilburn-Scott.

Another import about this time was Sam, owned by Miss Puxley. In 1910, the bitch Ayesha was imported from Nova Zembla in Siberia by Mr. Colman and Mr. Gray-Landsberg. Later she was sold to Mrs. Cammack. Ayesha was a pure white and, bred to males from the Kilburn-Scott's strains, produced many fine specimens.

In the 1920s Mrs. Gray-Landsberg acquired Pelle of Halfway. Later she imported Yugor of Halfway, who had excellent conformation but flop ears. Viga and Karloff were also imported during this time but were not used much for breeding.

Samoyeds were first exhibited in 1893 in the Foreign Dog Class. In 1901 the Kennel Club granted the breed registration privileges, and in 1909 gave the breed official recognition.

It was also in 1909 that Mrs. Kilburn-Scott and other early fanciers drew up the Standard for the Samoyed and made the decision to go with the white dog exclusively—discarding the brown, black, and spotted members of the breed. This entailed sacrifices because most of these fanciers either owned or had bred colored specimens, and there was at least one black and white champion—Ch. Alacbra. But the reasons they gave made sense: the majority of the dogs in the Siberian homeland were white; the colored dogs sometimes showed mongrel traits; and there was no medium-sized white long-haired bench show dog and a white Samoyed filled that niche.

The first Samoyed breed club, "The Samoyede Club," was formed in 1909, too. It was for male owners exclusively. The ladies formed their own club, "The Ladies Samoyede Club," in 1912. In 1920 the two groups merged to form the "Samoyed Association," sometimes referred to as the "Samoyed Association of Great Britain." Major Frederick Jackson served as President until his death in 1938.

Ch. Silver Moon, top producing brood bitch for 1963, 1964, and 1965. Owners, Bonnie and Bob Bowles.

Snowland sled team of Mrs. Helen Harris, 1939. Lead dog is Ch. Moscow of Farningham of Snowland (imported). At point are Ch. Nim of Snowland and Ch. Nadya of Snowland. At wheel are Ch. Sprint of the Arctic (imported) and Ch. Siberian Nansen of Farningham of Snowland (imported).

The Samoyed in America

Americans were introduced to the Samoyed by Mercy d'Argenteau, Princess de Montyglyon, a Belgian Countess and Hereditary Princess of the Holy Roman Empire. In 1902 while in Saint Petersburg for the dog show, the Princess saw and fell in love with a large Samoyed, Moustan, who was owned by the Grand Duke Michael, brother of Czar Nicholas II. The Princess hinted broadly, and later an enormous basket of orchids and roses with Moustan inside was delivered to her railway coach. It was a time of the grand gesture.

In 1904 the Princess immigrated to the States with Moustan, de Witte of Argenteau, Sora of Argenteau, and Martyska of Argenteau. Moustan was shown extensively and in 1906 became the first Samoyed to be registered with The American Kennel Club. Moustan's pedigree and background are mysteries, but he sired the first American champion, de Witte of Argenteau, who acquired the title in 1907. Ch. de Witte's dam was Sora of Argenteau, who was unregistered. Martyska of Argenteau (Houdin ex Olgalene) was from Mrs. Kilburn-Scott's kennels. In 1908, Siberia of Argenteau, another dog from the Princess's kennels, became the second champion.

In 1911 the Greenacre Kennels of Mrs. Ada Van Heusen got its start with the importation of Tamara, a daughter of Pedro (Peter the Great x Ch. Alaska) and Countess Thara (Nansen x Hecla). In 1915, Tamara became the fourth champion and the first champion bitch. She was bred to a son of de Witte and Martyska to produce Zuroff, who became the third champion in 1914 and was owned by V. W. Wertz; and, also, Ch. Greenacres Kieff, owned by John Cooper. In 1912 Mrs. Van Heusen imported Pasco, a daughter of Southern Cross, who was bred to Ch. Zuroff.

In 1914 Ruth Nichols acquired Wiemur, a bitch imported from England. Bred to Czarewitch, a son of de Witte and Martyska, Wiemur produced Ch. Malshick, whom Miss Nichols kept at her Top O' the World Kennels. Wiemur was also bred to a French import, Pompey, in whose pedigree appear Pedro and English Ch.

Alaska. In 1920 Miss Nichols acquired Trixie-Vera, an English import, from Mr. Girvan, who had bought her in 1917. Bred to Ch. Malshick, she produced the bitch Otiska, whose line continues today.

In 1915 Mrs. Frank Romer bought Sunny Ridge Pavlowa from John Cooper. She was a daughter of Ch. Greenacres Kieff and a granddaughter of Pasco and Ch. Zuroff. The next year Mrs. Romer acquired Ch. Shut Balackeror, a full brother of Ch. Malshick, from Ruth Nichols. With the acquisition of Otiska from Mr. Girvan, she had the base for her Yurak Kennels—excepting one.

That one—Tobolsk—arrived from England in 1920. He was a son of English Ch. Fang (Antarctic Buck x Kviklene) and Vilna (granddaughter of Southern Cross, Houdin, and English Ch. Pearlene). Line bred to Antarctic Buck, Tobolsk gave the American dogs much needed size and substance. The first of the three big imports of the 1920s, he finished his championship in 1921 and was much used for breeding. Tobolsk's litter sister Draga came over at the same time and finished her championship in 1922. Bred to Ch. Shut Balackeror, she produced Ch. Vilna of Yurak and Ch. Kritelka of Yurak. In the 1920s Mrs. Romer also imported from England Ch. Yurak's Nansen, Ch. Yurak's Trip of Farningham, and Ch. Maroosa of Farningham.

The Alfred Seeleys purchased their first Samoyed in 1917 from Mrs. Romer. This bitch, Ch. Zanoza, completed her championship in 1921. She was a daughter of Ch. Shut Balackeror and Sunny Ridge Pavlowa, and later the Seeleys acquired Olga of Yurak, another daughter of Ch. Shut out of Otiska. However, their Donerna Kennels are best known for their importation of Ch. Donerna's Barin, the second of the "biggies" of the 1920s. Barin was a son of English Ch. Kieff out of Ivanofna (a daughter of Antarctic Buck) and finished his title the same year he arrived—1922. Noted for his excellent gait and profuse coat, his influence in the breed was enormous, for he produced over one hundred puppies, including Ch. Brunoff, Ch. Vick, and others. In 1923 the Seeleys bought Barin's sister Donerna's Tsilma, who was in whelp to English Ch. Zahra. In this litter was Ch. Donerna's Ilinishna. Both Tsilma and her daughter finished their championships in 1924. Ch. Tsilma was bred to Ch. Nanook of Donerna (a son of Ch. Tobolsk) to produce Ch. Darya of Donerna and Ch. Norka of Donerna.

In 1920 Louis Smirnow bought his first dogs from Ella Fowler and Yurak Kennels. In 1922 he imported Olga of Farningham, who was in whelp to Polar Sea. In that litter was Ch. Yurak's Nansen, among others. That same year Mr. Smirnow imported Nico of Farningham, who was a champion by 1923.

Even with the many imports of the twenties, there was a general lack of uniformity and type, and dogs were often excused from the ring or refused ribbons because of their inferior quality—or the inferior quality of the judges. At least two dogs who later did become champions had been refused ribbons. At the base of the problem was the lack of a Standard.

In typical fashion, breeders and fanciers did not organize themselves until disaster struck. The blow fell on Saint Valentine's Day in 1923 at the Westminster Show. Samoyeds were judged by an Englishman, a Mr. Mitchell, who withheld the Reserve ribbons for both dogs and bitches, declaring that the eligible dogs were not purebred. Since at least three were recent English imports, the astonishment of those attending the show was enormous. Fanciers and breeders gathered together immediately after the judging and formed the Samoyed Club of America, and set up committees to write a constitution and a Standard and to see to the election of officers. Three months later the Samoyed Club of America, with Mr. Louis Smirnow as President, was approved for membership in The American Kennel Club. The Standard for the breed, patterned closely on the English breed Standard, was adopted by the A.K.C. at the same time. For years Mr. Mitchell was execrated, but his was a true Valentine's gift—a parent club and a Standard.

In 1925 Morgan Wing started at Wingbrook by importing Yukon Mit, the third of three "biggies" of the 1920s that established the style and soundness of American Samoyeds for many years to come. Yukon Mit, noted for his typiness, finished his championship in 1926. Among his progeny were Ch. Gorka and Ch. Mitboi.

Alfred Seeley was killed in an auto crash in 1925 and Mrs. Seeley did not feel equal to operating the kennels by herself, so the dogs were sold. Ch. Donerna's Barin, Ch. Donerna's Ilinishna, and others went to the H. N. Pinkhams of Laika Kennels. Ch. Tsilma and many of the other dogs went to the Arctic Kennels of Dr. Frank Dutton.

Martha Humphriss purchased her first Samoyed—Ch. Darya of Donerna—in 1925. That same year she acquired Ch. Zenaide, a daughter of Yurak's Nansen, but she purchased her most famous dog from Ella Fowler in 1926. He was Ch. Icy King, by a son of

American and Canadian Ch. Saroma's Polar Prince, a Best-in-Show and multiple Group winner, top producing Samoyed in 1964, and stud dog trophy winner in 1968 and 1971.

Ch. Silver Crest's Sikandi, foundation brood bitch of the Drayalene bloodline of Helene and Layard Spathold.

Ch. Kazan of Kentwood, owned by Bob and Dolly Ward, is pictured here playing ball, his favorite game which he played until the day before he died at nearly fifteen years of age.

Ch. Nico of Farningham x Lady Olga. These three were the base for the Siberian bloodlines. At one time Miss Humphriss had over a hundred dogs in her kennels.

In 1926 the Reids of Norka Kennels acquired Ch. Norka of Donerna from Mrs. Seeley. About the same time they bought Ch. Toby of Yurak II, already a champion, and Maroosa of Farningham, whom they finished to her championship. These two produced Ch. Norka's Lev, Ch. Norka's Dutschka, and Ch. Norka's Tasia; but the Reids' important dog was English Ch. Tiger Boy (a son of English Ch. Kara Sea), who was registered in the States as Tiger Boy of Norka in 1929. He was a fine stud dog and was Best of Breed at the first Samoyed Club of America Specialty. In 1930 the Reids imported Ch. Nooya of Norka, and in 1931, Ch. Zahrina of Norka.

By 1927 Mrs. J. C. McDowell had begun operations at her Khiva Kennels with Ch. Patricia Obi (a daughter of Tobolsk and Yurak's Zanada), Ch. Yancey's Daughter (a daughter of Tiger Boy and a granddaughter of Ch. Yukon Mit), and Nico of Creve (a son of Ch. Nico of Farningham). In 1931 she imported Ch. Snow Frost of the Arctic and White Countess of the Arctic. Among the dogs from her kennels were Ch. Jack Frost of Sacramento and Ch. Khiva's Matchika.

Miss Elizabeth Hudson had owned Samoyeds since before World War I, but in 1930 she imported one of the most influential dogs of the thirties—Ch. Storm Cloud. In 1934 she imported the bitch Morina of Taimur, and these two dogs, through their progeny, are influential in today's dogs.

On a trip to Europe in 1932, Mrs. Helen Harris and her daughter, Faith, saw their first Samoyed, and brought Pedlar of the Arctic back with them. Later, Mrs. Harris imported Sabarka and Sasha of Farningham, purchased from Mrs. Kilburn-Scott. In 1935 she purchased Ch. Ice Crystal of the Arctic, who was in whelp to English Ch. Leader of the Arctic. She also acquired Starshaya, a daughter of Ch. Storm Cloud and Ch. White Sprite of the Arctic, and Vida of Snowland, a daughter of Ch. Storm Cloud and Morina of Taimur. Then Mrs. Harris imported a puppy who became the influential Ch. Siberian Nansen of Farningham of Snowland, as well as Ch. Moscow of Farningham of Snowland and Ch. Sprint of the Arctic. These dogs were the foundation stock of the incomparable Snowland bloodlines.

Snowland dogs were shown by professional handler Nate

Ch. Ivan Belaya of Taymylyr, CD, owned by John and Carol Chittum and handled by them to several Best-of-Breed wins in tough California competition. He was also winner of the Stud Dog Class at the 1974 Samoyed Club of America Specialty.

Ch. Southern Star of Lynthea, bred and owned by James and Marian Osborn. Because of her importance as a brood bitch, Star has been shown sparingly since finishing.

Levine, and all were also trained for sled work. The Author once asked a Samoyed fancier (an owner of two Best-in-Show Samoyeds) about the Snowland dogs. "The Snowland dogs were gorgeous, just gorgeous! They had everything—soundness, gait, beauty, coat, marvelous heads, and good temperaments." And, indeed, ninety-five percent of today's Samoyeds who are winning regularly in the show ring go back to the Snowland dogs.

Mrs. Catherine Quereaux bought her first Samoyed in 1926 and owned several dogs throughout the years, but her real contribution was in the role of historian and critic. Until her death in the early 1950s, she wrote articles, analyzed pedigrees, and prodded breeders to avoid blindness to poor qualities of their dogs. In 1933 Miss Vera Lawrence began her Samoyed column in *Western Kennel World*. She, too, provided a sounding board for the fancy, and in her column began the publication of Mrs. Quereaux's history of the Samoyed "Dog of the Ages." Miss Lawrence owned, among others, Lenssen of Snowland.

Also active in the 1930s were Harry and Ada Yencer with their Darya Kennels, whose stock came from the Norka bloodlines; and Mrs. Horace Mann, whose imported Ch. White Sprite of the Arctic produced dogs sired by Ch. Gorka and Ch. Storm Cloud. Roy Brott's Arbee foundation dogs came from Siberian, Norka, and Mrs. Horace Mann, and he produced Ch. Vodka and Ch. Vodka's Snow Drift. He also owned and showed Ch. Zoveek of Snowland.

Mrs. Agnes Mason acquired Czar Nicholas Lenanov, later a champion, from M. D. Robinson in 1935, and purchased Dascha of Laika from the Pinkhams at Laika. In 1938 she bought Ch. Nianya of Snowland, and in 1939 she imported Ch. White Way of Kobe from Mrs. D. L. Perry's kennels in England and Silver Spark of the Arctic from Miss Keyte-Perry. These five dogs were the foundation stock of the White Way bloodlines. Mrs. Mason was an enthusiastic sled dog owner and her dogs were trained and raced by Lloyd Van Sickle. Mrs. Mason bred and owned Ch. Herdsman's Faith, Ch. Herdsman's Chattigan, Rex of White Way, and Ch. Petrof Lebanov. She was the breeder of many champions owned by others, including Ch. White Way's Juliet O'Snow Ridge, Ch. Silver Star of White Way, and Ch. Suzanne of White Way.

Pamela Rhanor began her Petsamo Kennels in the early 1940s with Tania of Petsamo of Khiva and Siberian stock. She acquired Ch. Khatanga of Snowland, Ch. White Christmas of Snowland, Ch. Silver Star of White Way, and, later, Sooltan and Ch. Kikmik of

Ch. Starchak, CD, pictured at fourteen months of age while visiting his breeders at White Way Kennels, Agnes and Aljean Mason. The 1956 Samoyed Club of America top producing stud dog, he was owned by Bob and Dolly Ward.

Ch. Vellee's Chayka, bred, owned, and handled by Duvella and Leland Kusler.

Oceanside. She produced foundation stock for many well-known breeders of later years.

In the 1940s the J. J. Marshalls acquired Ch. Yeinsei Czar Nicholas II and Ch. Frola of Snowland to start their Sammar bloodline. They owned Ch. Frolnick of Sammar and produced Sweet Missy of Sammar, the first Best-in-Show Samoyed. In Washington State Betty Ann Arneson acquired Ch. Kishie Choice Arneson in 1944, and later bought Snow King of Petsamo to produce the Betty Blue bloodlines which appear behind most of the dogs in the Northwest today, including Ch. Stormy Weather of Betty Blue (owned by the Gleasons), Ch. Chimi of Betty Blue, and Ch. Misty Way of Betty Blue.

In 1945 Billy Tucker bought Rhanor's Tynda of Petsamo and bred her to Ch. Starchak, of White Way bloodlines, to produce Ch. Kunto of Encino. Later, the Tuckers imported Suretta of Kobe in whelp to English Ch. Raff of Kobe. These dogs are the foundation of Kobe of Encino, which has produced some twenty champions. Mrs. Tucker is still active in breeding and exhibiting today.

The most spectacular import of the mid-forties was Ch. Martingate Snowland Taz, who was brought over by Dr. William Ivens. Taz was the sire of twenty-eight champions, and when Dr. Ivens retired in 1951, Taz went to Elma Miller at her Elkenglo Kennels.

Ruth Bates Young, who started with the kennel name Obi but later switched to Top-Acres, went to Breezewood and Arbee for foundation stock. Her Ch. Sparkle Plenty of Arbee, bred to Ch. Martingate Snowland Taz, produced Ch. Pratika, Ch. Narguess, and Ch. Hadesse of Top-Acres. For years she was the Samoyed columnist for *Popular Dogs* magazine.

Mrs. Bernice Ashdown had owned dogs for several years when she acquired Ch. Rimsky of Norka, who became the first U.D.T. Samoyed, but her Wychwood Kennels became nationally known with the importation of English Ch. Princess Silvertips of Kobe in 1949. This bitch was undefeated in England and quickly finished her American championship with a record of forty-eight Best-of-Breed wins, thirty-three Working Group placements, and two Best-in-Show wins. Bred to Ch. Martingate Snowland Taz, she produced Ch. Silver Spray of Wychwood and Ch. Silvertips Scion of Wychwood, both Best-in-Show winners. Their sister Ch. Silvertips Saba of Wychwood, the only Samoyed to win over her dam, was a Working Group winner many times.

Hazel and Bill Dawes began their Lucky Dee Samoyeds in 1948

American and Canadian Ch. Oakwood Farm's Kari J'Go Diko, owned by Leslie and Joan Lueck.

Ch. Silveracres Charm, owned by Harold and Doris McLaughlin.

Ch. Los Laika's Belaya Traicer, owned by Ed and Gertrude Adams.

with Ch. Lucky Labon Nahum, a male whose pedigree went back to Siberian, White Way, and Mrs. McDowell's dogs. Later, they acquired Ch. Faustina Fauna, of White Way and Sammar bloodlines. These two dogs plus a breeding to Suzanne's Raicer Suraine (of Snowland and White Way strains) were the foundation dogs at Lucky Dee, producing Ch. Vrai of Lucky Dee, a two-time Best-in-Show winning bitch; Ch. Modoc of Lucky Dee, Ch. Modette of Lucky Dee, Ch. White Beauty of Lucky Dee, Ch. Bunky of Lucky Dee, and others. Mr. and Mrs. Dawes sold dogs to the Breatchels, the Spatholds, Winford and Vera Messier, and others.

Jean Blank and Percy Matheron's Ch. Yurok of Whitecliff was whelped in 1955. A son of Ch. Omak and Kara Babkah of White Frost, Ch. Yurok equaled Ch. Silver Spray of Wychwood's record of five Best-in-Show wins, owner-handled by Mrs. Blank. His son Ch. Shoshone of Whitecliff, out of Ch. Nakomis of Whitecliff, was also a Best-in-Show winner.

Elma Miller of Elkenglo Kennels purchased Ch. Martingate Snowland Taz from Dr. Ivens in 1951 to breed to Frona of Blakewood and Ch. Ilma of Blakewood. She produced many champions sired by Taz.

In the early 1950s, Tom and Lucy Schneider purchased Taz's son Ch. Elkenglo's Jola. He was a top producing dog in the 1950s, as was his kennel mate, Ch. Lt's Lulo Luloto.

A spectacular winner of the 1950s was Ch. Nordly's Sammy, a grandson of Ch. Martingate Snowland Taz owned by Mr. and Mrs. John Doyle.

This same period saw an explosion of winning dogs in the Northwest from the Betty Blue bloodlines. Mr. and Mrs. Kenneth Kolb had Ch. Ken-Dor's Sky Komish and Ch. Ken-Dor's Pat Nak. John and Lila Wier's Joli Kennels began with Ch. Tod-Acres Fang, a son of Ch. Stormy Weather of Betty Blue, and Ch. Kobe's Nan-Nuk of Encino, purchased from Billie Tucker. Joli produced the Best-in-Show winning Ch. Joli Knika and Ch. Joli White Knight. Cliff and Nell Collins chose the kennel name Nichi, which means "of the best" in Eskimo. All their dogs were given Eskimo names, including Piu-Lengi-Nichi, Ch. Nipitluk Takoka of Nichi, Ch. Kapegah Okanok of Nichi, and others.

The Fitzpatricks' Ch. Sam O'Khan's Tsari of Khan (American and Canadian Ch. Zaysan of Krisland, C.D., x Ch. Whitecliff's Polar Dawn), mated with Bob and Bonnie Bowles' Ch. Noatak of Silver Moon, has produced many notable dogs: Ch. Sam O'Khan's

Tian Shan, Ch. Sam O'Khan's Sali Sarai, Ch. Sam O'Khan's Kubla Khan, Ch. Sam O'Khan's Khyber Khan, and Ch. Sam O'Khan's Chingis Khan, who was owned by Jim and Joan Sheets and has five Best-in-Show wins to his credit. Tsari won top producing brood bitch awards for 1966, 1967, 1968, and 1970.

The current record winning Samoyed, with six Best-in-Show wins, is American and Canadian Ch. Lulhaven's Snow Mist Ensign, who is from the Betty Blue strains and is owned by Sonny White and Ott Hyatt. Sired by Dick and Martha Beal's American and Canadian Ch. Saroma's Polar Prince, "Tiki" has six American and eighteen Canadian Best-in-Show wins.

Polar Prince (Ch. Tod-Acres Fang x Ch. Leordan's Taku Glacier) also sired American and Canadian Ch. Lulhaven's Nunatat, Ch. Cherski's Polar Koryak, and Ch. Lulhaven's Yakutat.

The Snow Ridge Kennels of Leona and Wade Powell were established with a pure strain of White Way from Agnes Mason. Ch. White Way's Juliet O'Snow Ridge, Ch. Patrice of Snow Ridge, and Ch. Snow Ridge's Ruble of Tamarack, owned by Madelin Druse, were from the Powells. The Powells were racing enthusiasts, and Madelin Druse is continuing in that field.

In the late 1950s Helen Spathold and her father, Layard, began with Ch. White Beauty of Lucky Dee. Adding White Frost from the Breatchels and Whitecliff from Jean Blank, Helen Spathold created the Drayalene strain. Ch. Silver Crest's Sikandi, her brood bitch, had the distinction of being the only Samoyed to win Best of Breed over Ch. Yurok of Whitecliff twice. Bred to Ch. Yurok, Sikandi produced Ch. Rokandi of Drayalene. "Rok" produced his best offspring when bred to Snow Ridge and White Way bitches, and from them came Ch. Patrice of Snow Ridge, a Group winner; Ch. Silver Snokandi; Ch. Drayalene's Rocotta of Kauzja; Ch. Sun Valley's Snow King, C.D.; and Ch. Nachalnik of Drayalene, the foundation stud dog of the Silveracres Kennels of Harold and Doris McLaughlin. Sikandi was also bred to Yurok's son Ch. Shoshone of Whitecliff to produce Ch. Barceia's Shondi of Drayalene, the foundation stud of Elliott Colburn's Ellbur strain.

After purchasing Ch. Nachalnik of Drayalene, the McLaughlins obtained Ch. Cnejinka, and these two are the foundation of the Silveracres Kennels, which have produced Ch. Silveracres Charm, a Group-winning bitch; Ch. Silveracres Rogue Kabri Vok; American and Canadian Ch. Silveracres Winter Chief; Ch. Silveracres Belaya

Chalinka, owned by the Russell Rogers; Ch. Silveracres Ivan; Ch. Silveracres Kantishna; and others. "Chiefie" was the Samoyed Club of America top stud dog for 1970, 1973, and 1974, and sired Ch. Kondako's Dancing Bear, also a Samoyed Club of America top stud dog in 1972 and 1975. "Chiefie" has produced thirty-four champion offspring. Among them is American and Canadian Ch. Kipperic Kandi of Suruka Orr, C.D., a bitch with two Best-in-Show wins as well as Best of Breed at the 1973 Specialty.

The Kondako Kennels of Connie and Dave Richardson carry on the Drayalene strain with Ch. Kondako's Dancing Bear. He has produced, among others, Ch. Kondako's Sun Dancer, Ch. Kondako's American Bear, and Ch. Kondako's Silver Sparkle.

Elliott Colburn of Ellbur Kennels has produced Ch. Snokandi's Hondo; Ch. Dudinka's Diva; American and Canadian Ch. Shaloon of Drayalene, owned by Pinehill Kennels; Ch. Shondra of Drayalene; Ch. Trina of Taymylyr; and others.

In the Midwest, Estelene Beckman, who has been very active in club work and served as President of the Samoyed Club of America, started her Frostar strain with Ch. Kusang of Northern Frost and Tundra Princess Starya, a daughter of Ch. Fronick of Sammar. Later she acquired Ch. Kymric Taz of Top-Acres, a son of Ch. Martingate Snowland Taz. Carrying on with the Frostar strain are Joyce and Louis Cain at Samtara Kennels. Their first was the bitch Ch. Frostar Tundra Star Frost. They have produced Ch. Samtara's Snow Gay Fantasy, Ch. Samtara's Karion Frost, Ch. Samtara's Sugay N'Spice, Ch. Samtara's Suga Daddi, and others.

Jean Baer at Baerstone has Ch. Stutz of Baerstone of Kobe, who is from Encino, Lucky Dee, and Snowland bloodlines. From Baerstone have come Ch. Baerstone's Kasija, Ch. Honey Baer-Stone of Grow of Gro-Wil, and Ch. Bopper El Toro of Baerstone, among others.

The late 1960s saw the death of Miss Juliet Goodrich of Snowshoe Hill, for many years an ardent fancier and publicist for the breed. From her estate a substantial trust fund was set up to continue her work with dogs. The trustees have instituted the awarding of a special medallion to all dogs finishing their championships and obedience titles. Among other good works of the Juliet Goodrich Trust Fund are the top winners and top producers awards, and a pamphlet on Samoyeds for the education of new and prospective owners.

Best-of-Breed winning Ch. Celestial Karma of Darius, owned and handled by Carol Yhlen.

Ch. Aladdin's Silver Snowstorm with his handler, ten-year-old John Pokora. This team of dog and child has made young John one of the top Junior Handlers in the country.

Ch. Barceia's Shondi of Drayalene, owned by Elliott Colburn.

Dr. Leslie and Joan Lueck of Oakwood Farms purchased Ch. Velko of Chipaquipa, from Top-Acres, and Ch. Silveracres Ivan, a son of Ch. Nachalnik of Drayalene. Their Group winner is Ch. Oakwood Farm's Kari J'Go Diko (Ch. Sam O'Khan's Chingis Khan x American and Canadian Ch. Oakwood Farm's Silver Kari). John and Joan Scovin at Weathervane Kennels selected stock from Whitecliff's Polar Dawn, Tara's Snow Boy (a grandson of Ch. Martingate Snowland Taz), and strains from Joli. They are producing current winners with Ch. Siayes Schnegora Boickh, Ch. Taradawn's Bereskova, American and Canadian Ch. Karatyll's Tia of Weathervane, and Ch. Taradawn's Snow Princess, among others.

Mrs. Duvella Kusler's Ch. Vellee's Chayka has a spectacular record, and the Vellee Kennels continue to produce winners from Drayalene and Northwest bloodlines. John and Evelyn Coloma own dogs from Mrs. Kusler's bloodlines, including Ch. Reddison of Vellee, Best of Opposite Sex at the 1973 Specialty.

Dennis and Gretchen Raymond's Williwaw Kennels produce sound dogs consistently. Their strain goes back to Ch. Omak and Kobe of Encino. The Raymonds have produced Ch. Buddy Boy of Williwaw, Ch. Mister Williwaw, Ch. Snow Trek's Mister Teddy, Ch. Kelly of Williwaw, Ch. White Tundra's Williwaw Sue, and others. Both Carole Barnum of Sassillie Kennels and Barbara and Mako Yamasaki of Rickshaw strains acquired their basic stock from Williwaw.

Carol and John Chittum have amalgamated strains from Drayalene, Snow Ridge, and Ch. Kazan of Kentwood with their Ch. Ivan Belaya of Taymylyr, C.D., and Ch. Anja Belaya Petroushka, to produce their Belaya Samoyeds. Among their winners is Ch. Los Laik's Belaya Traicer, owned by Edwin and Gertrude Adams, who have owned and exhibited Samoyeds since the very early days.

In the early days of the Samoyed fancy, kennels were large and owners hired full-time professional handlers and kennel help. Today's average breeder keeps fewer than eight dogs and a large kennel keeps only twenty or so. The impetus for help for the beginner in the fancy has been taken up by the local Samoyed breed clubs, which provide a nucleus of expertise, and whose members can provide first-hand information on training, exhibiting, and general care.

Ch. Kobe's Komak of Encino, whelped in 1955 and bred and owned by Billie Tucker.

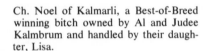

Ch. Noel of Kalmarli, a Best-of-Breed winning bitch owned by Al and Judee Kalmbrum and handled by their daughter, Lisa.

Best-of-Breed winning bitch, Ch. Kobe's Katyushka of Encino, owned by Dick and Sandy Hopson.

Samoyed Club of America Trophy Winners

In the 1950s four perpetual trophies were instituted for top winning Samoyeds owned by members of the Samoyed Club of America. They were the A. E. Mason Memorial Trophy for top winning dog, the Ch. Suzanne of White Way Memorial Trophy for top winning bitch, the Wimundstrev Trophy for top stud dog, and the Charles Tucker Memorial Trophy for top brood bitch. The stud dog and brood bitch trophies were awarded on the basis of points won by progeny during the year with extra points for championships completed and Working Group placements.

In 1969 the perpetual trophies were retired and new awards were instituted by the Samoyed Club of America, financed by the Juliet Goodrich Trust Fund. Besides the categories of top winners and top producers, a new award for Top Obedience Winner was added. Only dogs owned by members of the Samoyed Club of America are eligible.

Top Winning Samoyed Dog

1956 Ch. King of Wal-Lyn—Smith
1957 Ch. King of Wal-Lyn—Smith
1958 Ch. Yurok of Whitecliff—Blank and Matheron
1959 Ch. Yurok of Whitecliff—Blank and Matheron
1960 Ch. Yurok of Whitecliff—Blank and Matheron
1961 Ch. Shoshone of Whitecliff—Blank
1962 Ch. Winterland's Kim—Heagy
1963 Ch. Noatak of Silver Moon—Bowles
1964 Ch. Saroma's Polar Prince—Beal
1965 Ch. Kara Sea's Silver Nikki—Gowdyk
1966 Ch. Sam O'Khan's Chingis Khan—Sheets
1967 Ch. Sam O'Khan's Chingis Khan—Sheets
1968 Ch. Sam O'Khan's Chingis Khan—Sheets
1969 Ch. Sam O'Khan's Chingis Khan—Sheets
1970 Ch. Sam O'Khan's Chingis Khan—Sheets
1971 Am., Can., and Bmd. Ch. Lulhaven's Snowmist Ensign—Hyatt and White
1972 Ch. Czar's Dorak of Whitecliff—Walker
1973 Eng., Am., and Can. Ch. Delmonte This Is It—Houten
1974 Am. and Can. Ch. North Starr King's Ransom—Hritzo
1975 Am. and Can. Ch. North Starr King's Ransom—Hritzo

Top Winning Samoyed Bitch

1959 Ch. Ell-Tee Roxanne—Schneider
1960 Ch. Ell-Tee Roxanne—Schneider
1961 Ch. Frostar's Tundra Starfrost—Cain
1962 Ch. Frostar's Tundra Starfrost—Cain
1963 Ch. Frostar's Princess Snowball—Lawton
1964 Ch. Chu-San's Mei Ling O'Yeniseisk—Dendinger
1965 Ch. Samtara's Sugay'N Spice—Cain
1966 Ch. Dudinka's Diva—Noland and Eaton
1967 Ch. Ka-Tag's Memory in Silver—Tagliaferri and Dendinger
1968 Ch. Ka-Tag's Memory in Silver—Tagliaferri and Dendinger
1969 Ch. Honey Babe of Gro-Wil—Walls
1970 Ch. Orion's Mishka of Marcomar—Eggiman
1971 Int., Am., Can., and Mex. Ch. Babe's Gypsy Magic of Gro-Will—Dewey
1972 Am. and Can. Ch. Kipperic Kandi of Suruka Orr, C.D.—Hodges
1973 Am. and Can. Ch. Kipperic Kandi of Suruka Orr, C.D.—Hodges
1974 Am. and Can. Ch. Kipperic Kandu of Suruka Orr, C.D.—Hodges
1975 Am. and Can. Ch. Bubbles LaRue of Oakwood—Price

Top Producing Samoyed Stud Dog

1954 Ch. Martingate Snowland Taz—Miller
1955 Ch. Martingate Snowland Taz—Miller
1956 Ch. Starchak, C.D.—Ward
1957 Ch. Omak—Matheron
1958 Ch. Stormy Weather of Betty Blue—Gleason
1959 Ch. Elkenglo's Jola—Schneider
1960 Ch. Elkenglo's Jola—Schneider
1961 Ch. Yurok of Whitecliff—Blank and Matheron
1962 Am. and Can. Ch. Tod-Acres Fang—Weir
1963 Ch. Elkenglo's Jola—Schneider
1964 Am. and Can. Ch. Tod-Acres Fang—Weir
1965 Am. and Can. Ch. Noatak of Silver Moon—Bowles
1966 Am. and Can. Ch. Noatak of Silver Moon—Bowles
1967 Am. and Can. Ch. Noatak of Silver Moon—Bowles
1968 Am. and Can. Ch. Noatak of Silver Moon—Bowles
1969 Am. and Can. Ch. Saroma's Polar Prince—Beal
1970 Ch. Nachalnik of Drayalene—McLaughlin
1971 Am. and Can. Ch. Saroma's Polar Prince—Beal
1972 Ch. Kondako's Dancing Bear—Richardson
1973 Ch. Nachalnik of Drayalene—McLaughlin
1974 Ch. Nachalnik of Drayalene—McLaughlin
1975 Ch. Kondako's Dancing Bear—Richardson

Top Producing Samoyed Brood Bitch

1953 Ch. Modoc of Lucky Dee—Long
1954 Ch. Faustina Fauna—Dawes
1955 Ch. Sparkle Plenty of Arbee—Young
1956 Ch. Frola of Snowland—Marshall
1957 Ch. Vrai of Lucky Dee—Dawes
1958 Ch. Lt's Lulo Luloto—Schneider
1959 Ch. Sparkle Plenty of Arbee—Young
1960 Tundra Princess Starya—Beckman
1961 Am. and Can. Ch. Kobe's Nan-Nuk of Encino—Weir
1962 Tundra Princess Starya—Beckman
1963 Ch. Silver Moon—Bowles
1964 Ch. Silver Moon—Bowles
1965 Ch. Silver Moon—Bowles
1966 Am. and Can. Ch. Sam O'Khan's Tsari of Khan—Fitzpatrick
1967 Am. and Can. Ch. Sam O'Khan's Tsari of Khan—Fitzpatrick
1968 Am. and Can. Ch. Sam O'Khan's Tsari of Khan—Fitzpatrick
1969 Ch. Tempest of Misty Way—McCarthy
1970 Am. and Can. Ch. Sam O'Khan's Tsari of Khan—Fitzpatrick
1971 Ch. Honey Babe of Gro-Wil—Baer
1972 Silver Sonnett of Gro-Wil—Baer
1973 Ch. Kim's Lady Bug—Lycan
1974 Ch. Silver Trinkets of Misty Way—McCarthy
1975 Ch. Silver Trinkets of Misty Way—McCarthy

Top Obedience Samoyed

1969 Ch. Snowline's Joli Shashan, C.D.X.—Mayfield
1970 Ell-Tee's Square Do Tasha, U.D.—Gormley
1971 Snowman of Whitehall, U.D.—Smith
1972 Snowman of Whitehall, U.D.—Smith
1973 Silver Charm of Starfire, U.D.—Decker
1974 Ch. Tsarevich of Kobray, U.D.—Ruby
1975 White Glamour of Starfire, U.D.—Decker

Three generations of champion bitches at Samtara: Ch. Frostar's Tundra Star Frost, Ch. Samtara's Snow Gay Fantasy, and Ch. Samtara's Sugay N'Spice. Owned and handled by Joyce and Louis Cain.

Lucky Dee sled team of Bill and Hazel Dawes at a Navy Christmas party in 1953. Lead dog, Ch. Lucky Labon Nahum; right point, Ch. Vrai of Lucky Dee; left point, Ch. Faustina Fauna; at wheel, Ch. Bai of Lucky Dee and Ch. Modette of Lucky Dee.

Christmas with Mrs. Agnes Mason and her daughter, Aljean. From left, Duke of White Way, Ch. Herdsman's Victory Leader, and the imported Ch. White Way of Kobe.

Ch. Yurok of Whitecliff, top winning Samoyed in 1958, 1959, and 1960, and top producing stud dog in 1961. Owned by Jean Blank and Percy Matheron.

The Samoyed Club of America currently holds Specialty Shows on a yearly basis. In some earlier years no Specialty Show was held, and in other years more than one was held.

1929 Ch. Tiger Boy of Norka—Reid
1930 Ch. Storm Cloud—Hudson
1937 Krasan—Keegan
1938 Ch. Norka's Moguiski—Foster
1939 Ch. Prince Kofski—Ruick
1940 Ch. Prince Igor II—Keegan
1941 Ch. Alstasia's Rukavitza, C.D.—McBain
1946 Ch. Frolnick of Sammar—Marshall
1947 Ch. Staryvna of Snowland—Ward
1948 Ch. Gay of White Way—Mason
1950 Ch. Verla's Prince Comet—Hill
1952 Ch. Verla's Prince Comet—Hill
1953 Ch. Zor of Altai—Ruth
1954 Ch. King of Wal-Lynn—Smith
1955 Ch. Tazson's Snow Flicka—Ulfeng
     Ch. Polaris Pan—Klein and Mueller
1956 Ch. Bunky Jr. of Lucky Dee—Dawes
     Ch. Nordly's Sammy—Doyle
1957 Ch. Nordly's Sammy—Doyle
1958 Ch. Nordly's Sammy—Doyle
1959 Ch. Nordly's Sammy—Doyle
1960 Ch. Shoshone of Whitecliff—Blank
1962 Ch. Elkenglo's Dash O'Silver—Miller
1963 Ch. Winterland's Kim—Heagy
1964 Ch. Sarges Silver Frost—Parry
     Ch. Shondra of Drayalene—Dyer
1965 Ch. Shaloon of Drayalene—Wacenske
     Ch. Winter Kloud of Silver Moon—Helinski
     Ch. Kenny's Blazer Boy of Caribou, C.D.X.—Yocum
     Ch. Snowpack Silver Melody of Kobe—Ashdown
     Ch. Danlyn's Silver Coronet—Torres
1966 Ch. Park-Cliffe Snowpack Sanorka, C.D.—McGoldrick
     Ch. Sayan of Woodland—Kite
1967 Ch. Venturer of Kobe—Jordan
     Ch. Star Nika Altai of Silver Moon—Miller
     Ch. Sayan of Woodland—Kite
1969 Ch. Sayan of Woodland—Kite
1970 Ch. Darius Karlak Cheetal—Morgan
1971 Ch. Elrond Czar of Rivendell, C.D.—Gaffney
1972 Ch. Midnight Sun Kimba—Horton and Mandale
1973 Ch. Kipperic Kandu of Suruka Orr, C.D.—Hodges
1974 Ch. Stormy of Misty Way—McCarthy and Baird
1975 Ch. Frostymorn's Big Blizzard—Bartz
1976 Am. and Can. Ch. Oakwood Farm's Kari J'Go Diko—Lueck

Snokandi's Flicka, pictured at three years of age. Samoyeds learn tricks easily if they are praised and are rewarded liberally with tidbits of food.

A Very Special Personality

A Samoyed is just not everybody's kind of dog—not only because of the bother of his long coat. He is loving, gentle, friendly, and devoted to his family, but he is not naturally well-behaved, being too clever and too easily bored to lie about like a plush rug. He has a distinctive personality which is marked by super-dog intelligence. One Samoyed breeder has threatened for years to give prospective puppy buyers an I.Q. test to ensure that the owners are smarter than the dog they intend to buy.

Intelligence does not necessarily equal trainability. A Samoyed will learn quickly, but then it becomes a struggle of wills to get him to do *what* you want him to do *when* you want him to do it. If your Sam likes obedience work, he will be a superb performer. If not, do not plan on earning an obedience title—although all Samoyeds should have obedience training. Interest in obedience work is definitely a hereditary trait, so if you want a Sam for obedience, buy a puppy whose parents have obedience titles.

The next element of Samoyed personality is independence. Most Samoyeds, by the time they are two years old, have their human families trained beautifully. The dogs are very sweet and loving about it, and their families seem happy and usually unaware that the dog is the boss.

This combination of intelligence and independence can be wearing on an owner's patience. A Sam is easily bored, and if the action in his own yard is slow, he will seek excitement elsewhere and you will have a runaway on your hands. Of, if the yard is escape proof (which is doubtful with any Sam), he may take to chewing up trees and patio furniture to add spice to his life.

There are two ways to cure a bored, destructive escape artist. One is to allow him to spend more time with his family. Almost any outdoor activity that humans enjoy can be taken up with enthusiasm by a Samoyed. Paco, owned by John Bartelmez, goes sailing on San Francisco Bay nearly every week end and his sea manners are perfect. Roberta Flora's Tammie accompanies her mistress to her florist's shop every day, and Tammie has a coterie of admirers who drop by regularly to give her a tidbit and a hug.

Pooh Bear of Kauzja and young friend, Tiffany Zarate. Samoyeds can be trusted with very small children, but all children must learn to treat a dog properly and gently. That includes not pounding roughly, not poking fingers in eyes and ears, not pulling whiskers and hairs, and not picking up puppies.

The other solution is to buy another Samoyed to keep the first one company. Two Sams will play games of "keep away" and "king of the mountain" for hours, and be perfectly content.

The third special element in the Samoyed personality is his primitive, atavistic nature. The Author's Randi is as superb a mouser as any cat, and will spend hours waiting for a gopher to pop his head out of a hole. Some Sams are snake, lizard, and squirrel experts. Helen Spathold's Rokandi effectively protected his mistress from an errant rattlesnake and killed it, and Harold and Doris McLaughlin's Nachalnik catches chipmunks and squirrels.

Sams get along beautifully with other animals that are members of the family. Mrs. Kille's Tari adopted her housemate's litter of kittens after the mother cat had been killed, even diapering them and allowing them to nurse. But woe to the strange cat who has had fun teasing any Sam, because when the day comes that the cat miscalculates and is caught, he is a sure candidate for cat heaven. Sams are also anathema to chickens, ducks, and sheep.

The primitive strain also breaks through with bitches at whelping time. Closets and dark corners become the den or "hidey hole" the bitch would prepare for her puppies in the wild, and are always preferred to a specially prepared whelping box. Juno spent several days preparing her nest, and her owner, Kathy Nelson, was caught off guard, so Juno whelped three puppies in the L-shaped den she dug in the ground before she was "rescued" and returned to a civilized nursery to deliver the rest of the litter.

Samoyeds have demonstrated an amazing ability to survive in the wild or in an unfamiliar environment. Pat Murray's Sarina, a pampered show dog, was stolen and somehow escaped from her dognapers and was making her way home when she was distracted by a love affair. She whelped her puppies in a den in the woods and had raised them to four weeks of age when she was found by a neighboring farm family who returned her to her distraught owner—thanks to the dog's tattoo identification.

Years ago in the High Sierras during the winter, Mrs. Agnes Mason's Romeo was taken for a long romp in the snow. When the weather turned stormy and snow began to fall, Romeo's people prepared to return to the lodge and whistled for the dog, but he did not return. The blizzard continued all night, and the next morning when the weather cleared, a search party was organized. They tramped in the woods, searching and calling, most of the day. Just as they were about to give up and go home, a nearby drift began

Five-month-old Anatares Tatiana checks out dishes for any extra scraps and tastes.

An outdoor watering device for dogs which attaches to an outside spigot. These three-month-old puppies bred and owned by Tom and Mary Mayfield have learned to use the device and always have clean, fresh water to drink.

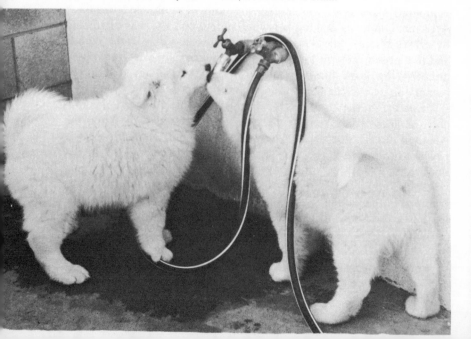

heaving and out popped Romeo. He had dug a hole and curled up, tail over nose, snug and out of the storm, and was none the worse for the experience.

Family protection comes high on a Sam's list of priorities. Doug and Linda Balcomb and their family and Christi and her son were camping in Southern Oregon when a cougar decided to investigate their camp. Christi and Specks had never seen anything wilder than a sparrow, but they chased the cougar off the roof of the camper and up a tree. The frightened Balcombs managed to drag the enraged dogs into the camper and shut the door, while the cougar gratefully hurried off into the night.

No less protective was Joe and Joanne Marineau's Larissa during a camping trip in the Sierras. As a train of pack horses appeared over the ridge, Larissa began stealthily to stalk these creatures until they approached her family's camping site. Then she planted herself resolutely in the middle of the trail and brought the whole string to a halt. She refused to let them pass until the Marineaus picked her up bodily and carried her back to camp.

Samoyeds are extremely careful with toddlers and will put up with an enormous amount of pestering and mauling. At the point when other dogs snap or bite, a Samoyed will, with great dignity, find a safe place away from the commotion.

The family Sam often feels the children are his special charges. Ernie and Wanda Ivaldi's Miss Lee decided she had had enough of a familiar adult neighbor wrestling and roughhousing with her boy, and she stopped it all with a smart nip on the neighbor's leg. Any parent who spanks a child had best do it out of sight of the family Sam, or the parent is likely to get a toothy reminder of who is first on the dog's list of VIPs.

Samoyeds are friendly dogs who genuinely like people, so their owners are always surprised when they display guard-dog behavior. A Sam does not like strangers around his family, his house, or his car; but people his family likes and accepts he will sensibly like and accept also.

The average Sam can be a hole digging, furniture chewing, noisy, greedy, atavistic demon. He can also be an extremely gentle, sensible, responsive, and loving companion. He seems to behave better as he gets older and gets his family trained to treat him as an equal. He is utterly charming and disarming, but there is one danger: once you have lived with a Sam, he will ruin you for any dog but another Samoyed.

Three-dog Samoyed team owned by Madelin Druse at the races in the Sierras. At lead is Ch. Snow Ridge's Ruble of Tamarack. At left wheel is his brother, Ch. Tyson's Rebel of Snow Ridge. At right wheel is their sire, Ch. Prince Tyson of Snow Ridge.

The Samoyed as a Working Dog

Samoyeds have been trained and used successfully for almost every type of work dogs can do except as war dogs. At the beginning of World War II, several Samoyeds were donated to the U.S. Army to be trained and used as attack dogs. They failed miserably, but they were used as sled dogs and messengers in the Arctic. Several Samoyeds were even trained to be dropped by parachute for rescue work.

Samoyeds have been trained and used as hunting dogs, too. Their eyesight and hearing are particularly keen, and they are excellent squirrel dogs.

Their coats require too much attention for Samoyeds to be used much as guide dogs for the blind, although they possess the sensitivity, intelligence, and sensible independence needed to make a good guide dog. Several Samoyeds have been trained and used as guide dogs very successfully, but they were trained privately for blind owners who had families willing to take care of the dogs' grooming needs.

Samoyeds do very well as pack animals. A dog pack, made of cotton webbing, consists of a body strap with a buckle, a chest strap, and a breech strap around the rear of the dog. The load must be carefully balanced on either side, for a dog supports the weight of the load over his back.

Obedience training was begun, as so many other things in dogdom, in England, and spread to the States and Canada in the 1930s. The first Samoyed to earn a Companion Dog title was Ch. Alstasia's Rukavitz, who was owned by Mrs. Anastasia MacBain and acquired the title in 1940. His granddaughter Ch. Marina of Wychwood, owned by Mrs. Ashdown, was the first Samoyed bitch to earn a Companion Dog title and the first bitch to earn a Companion Dog Excellent title. Mrs. Ashdown also owned Ch. Rimsky of Norka, who became the first Samoyed to earn the C.D.X. title and the first Samoyed to earn the Utility Dog Tracker title. Ch. Vojak of Samoyland, owned by Chloe and Tom Witcher, was one of the first Samoyeds to earn the Utility Dog title.

Shontara's Tara of Snow Fire, CDX, owned and trained by Marjorie Chiono, goes over the high jump.

The Mason's White Way sled team with Rex of White Way at left.

Here, Shontara's Tara of Snow Fire, CDX, practices for her next obedience degree.

Margie Couch has two obedience Sams she works as a brace. The dogs do the exercises as a team, even fetching and taking the hurdles and jumps together.

Sledding is the Samoyed's forte. Samoyeds love the snow and seem almost to have a racial memory of it. Even a Samoyed who has always lived in a temperate climate knows instinctively how to make his way through deep powder snow.

The premier Samoyed sled dog was Rex of White Way. He was owned by Agnes Mason, but he really belonged to Lloyd Van Sickle, his trainer and driver. Rex was a real working lead dog and earned his keep when Van Sickle had a U.S. mail contract in the backwoods of Idaho. Rex's parachute training came in handy, too, and he and the team once had to leave a dog show to rescue those aboard a downed plane in the Sierras. Rex racked up eleven points toward his championship, and his weight pulling record for the most pounds per pound of dog still stands.

Deputy Sheriff Harry Johannson, whose beat was the Sierras in the region of Lake Tahoe, used only Samoyeds in his sled teams. Johannson, now in his eighties and retired, still insists that anybody who has to rely on a dog team for all-purpose transportation in the wilderness should use nothing but Samoyeds. Several old-time trappers in the Canadian wilderness have agreed with him.

Today, rescue teams have been replaced by helicopters and snow tractors, but sled dog races go on. Sled races are run on elapsed time, and there are several classes: a junior class for children, three-dog races which go about three miles, five-dog races which go about eight miles, and an open class in which the driver may use as many dogs as he can hitch and handle, and which runs for ten or twenty miles. Racing clubs often hold classes for weight pulling and lead dog competition, also.

Lloyd and Ken Bristol and Ralph and Bev Ward have run large Samoyed teams and have done well. Bob LeCouer has used a mixed team of Samoyeds and has also done well.

Today's mushers are very vocal about the show ring ruining the Samoyed for his proper work, but the Author knows of four recent champions who have taken points and Best-of-Breed awards with harness marks in their coats.

Racing dogs must be kept in lean, hard condition and worked out two or three times a week, twelve months a year. This schedule keeps the driver in the same shape—which is important, for dog driving is strenuous work. Snow is not necessary, for the dogs can

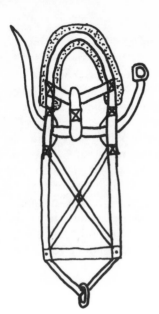

Harness, top view.

Harness, side view.

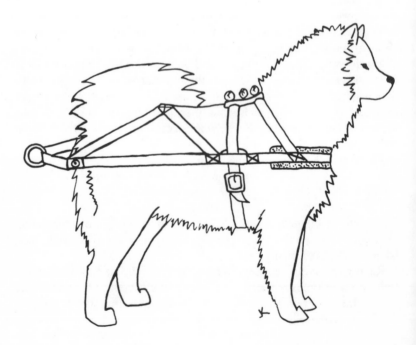

be hitched to a wheeled cart, or chassis, during the off-snow months. Some racing clubs even hold cart races in the summer.

A large stable of dogs is not required in order to have fun with draft work. The owner of one Samoyed can have a great deal of enjoyment by carting around the neighborhood or by skijoring— which is having the dog pull the skier over snow or ice. A lot of expensive equipment is not necessary, but a good harness is required. Illustrated here is an all-purpose harness you can make easily at home. It is not a racing harness. You will need:

Five yards of two-inch cotton webbing (not nylon).

Piece of wood three-quarters inch square and twelve inches long for the spreader, with a hole drilled in each end.

Two wood screws and washers.

Metal ring two and a half or three inches in diameter.

Buckle.

Carpet thread and large needle.

Padding material for breast strap.

Large safety pins.

Measure the webbing on the dog and pin the joints. When the fitting is completed, you can sew the joints or take the harness to a cobbler to be stitched.

First measure the length of webbing that goes around the dog's torso and make sure it rides forward far enough. Allow enough length to attach the buckle. Then measure the long strip that forms the breast strap and the side tugs. Allow enough material behind to double the webbing where the ring will ride. Bring the neck strap well forward at the top and sides so that it keeps the breast strap high and at the base of the neck in front. The breast strap must not weigh on the forelegs. In measuring the straps over the rump, be sure they will hold the spreader up into the feathering, so it will not bump the dog's rear legs when he moves. Thread the ring on the webbing, doubling it, and use the screws to fasten the webbing to the spreader. Pad the breast strap with several thicknesses of wool, felt, or sheepskin.

For draft work, do *not* use a metal choke collar. Use a leather collar or wide cloth no-choke collar.

Do not attach the harness directly to the cart. Instead, use a three-foot tow line with a large metal bolt snap at each end, and fasten one end to the ring on the harness and the other to the load. A child's wagon can be adapted for pulling by removing the tongue, but a braking device must be added. When the dog comes to an abrupt stop, a wagon, even loaded, will roll forward and bump the dog's rear. A couple of accidents like that and the dog will be ruined for draft work. A claw brake worked with the foot is best.

Most Samoyeds love pulling and take to it readily, but they do need coaxing and lots of praise. An old automobile tire or a large length of wood is good for beginning training in pulling. Attach a long rope to the dog's collar to guide him, because he must learn to move out ahead of you, steadily and evenly, not stopping to investigate the bushes or lift his leg.

"Hi" or "hup"—not "mush"—is the command to go. "Whoa" is for the halt. "Gee" is for a right turn and "haw" is for a left turn.

After each workout, always check your dog's pads for cuts or bruises. If you live in a neighborhood where dogs are permitted to run loose, it is a good idea to carry a large, flat, leather horse-quirt for protection when you are out mushing. The dog pulling is too busy to pick a fight, but he may be set upon by a loose dog.

Do *not* load up the cart with a heavy load and then keep adding to it just to see how much weight your dog can pull! Weight pulling requires a special harness, very special training, and knowledge far beyond the scope of this book.

Sled dogs must have year-round training. Here the K-Way sled team of Bob and Wanda Krauss is seen working out in a Wisconsin corn field with a gig on wheels. At lead is Prairiewind's Little Cindy, CD; at left point, Ch. K-Way's Gazelle; at right point, K-Way's Jeremiah Johnson; at left swing, K-Way's Touch of Class; at right swing, Kahlua of K-Way; at left wheel, Ch. Prairiewind's Shanna, CD; and at right wheel, K-Way's Mickey Finn. Jeremiah Johnson, Touch of Class, Kahlua, and Mickey Finn are litter mates.

Manners for the Family Dog

Although each dog has personality quirks and idiosyncrasies that set him apart as an individual, dogs in general have two characteristics that can be utilized to advantage in training. The first is the dog's strong desire to please, which has been built up through centuries of association with man. The second lies in the innate quality of the dog's mentality. It has been proved conclusively that while dogs have reasoning power, their learning ability is based on a direct association of cause and effect, so that they willingly repeat acts that bring pleasant results and discontinue acts that bring unpleasant results. Hence, to take fullest advantage of a dog's abilities, the trainer must make sure the dog understands a command, and then reward him when he obeys and correct him when he does wrong.

Commands should be as short as possible and should be repeated in the same way, day after day. Saying "Heel," one day, and "Come here and heel," the next will confuse the dog. *Heel, sit, stand, stay, down,* and *come* are standard terminology, and are preferable for a dog that may later be given advanced training.

Tone of voice is important, too. For instance, a coaxing tone helps cajole a young puppy into trying something new. Once an exercise is mastered, commands given in a firm, matter-of-fact voice give the dog confidence in his own ability. Praise, expressed in an exuberant tone, will tell the dog quite clearly that he has earned his master's approval. On the other hand, a firm "No" indicates with equal clarity that he has done wrong.

Rewards for good performance may consist simply of praising lavishly and petting the dog, although many professional trainers use bits of food as rewards. Tidbits are effective only if the dog is hungry, of course. And if you smoke, you must be sure to wash your hands before each training session, for the odor of nicotine is repulsive to dogs. On the hands of a heavy smoker, the odor of nicotine may be so strong that the dog is unable to smell the tidbit.

Correction for wrong-doing should be limited to repeating "No," in a scolding tone of voice or to confining the dog to his bed. Spanking or striking the dog is taboo—particularly using sticks, which might cause injury, but the hand should never be used either. For field training as well as some obedience work, the hand is used to signal the dog. Dogs that have been punished by slapping have a tendency to cringe whenever they see a hand raised and consequently do not respond promptly when the owner's intent is not to punish but to signal.

Some trainers recommend correcting the dog by whacking him with a rolled-up newspaper. The idea is that the newspaper will not injure the dog but that the resulting noise will condition the dog to avoid repeating the act that seemingly caused the noise. Many authorities object to this type of correction, for it may result in the dog's becoming "noise-shy"—a decided disadvantage with show dogs which must maintain poise in adverse, often noisy, situations. "Noise-shyness" is also an unfortunate reaction in field dogs, since it may lead to gun-shyness.

To be effective, correction must be administered immediately, so that in the dog's mind there is a direct connection between his act and the correction. You can make voice corrections under almost any circumstances, but you must never call the dog to you and then correct him, or he will associate the correction with the fact that he has come and will become reluctant to respond. If the dog is at a distance and doing something he shouldn't, go to him and scold him while he is still involved in wrong-doing. If this is impossible, ignore the offense until he repeats it. Then correct him properly.

Especially while a dog is young, he should be watched closely and stopped before he gets into mischief. All dogs need to do a certain amount of chewing, so to prevent your puppy's chewing something you value, provide him with his own balls and toys. Never allow him to chew cast-off slippers and then expect him to differentiate between cast-off items and those you value. Nylon stockings, wooden articles, and various other items may cause intestinal obstructions if the dog chews and swallows them, and death may result. Rubber and plastic toys may also be harmful if they are of types the dog can bite through or chew into pieces and then swallow. So it is essential that the dog be permitted to chew only on bones or toys he cannot chew up and swallow.

Serious training for obedience should not be started until a dog is a year old. But basic training in house manners should begin the day the puppy enters his new home. A puppy should never be given the run of the house but should be confined to a box or small pen except for play periods when you can devote full attention to him. The first thing to teach the dog is his name, so that whenever he hears it, he will immediately come to attention. Whenever you are near his box, talk to him, using his name repeatedly. During play periods, talk to him, pet him, and handle him, for he must be conditioned so he will not object to being handled by a veterinarian, show judge, or family friend. As the dog investigates his surroundings, watch him carefully and if he tries something he shouldn't, reprimand him with a scolding "No!" If he repeats the offense, scold him and confine him to his box, then praise him. Discipline must be prompt, consistent, and always followed with praise. Never tease the dog, and never allow others to do so. Kindness and understanding are essential to a pleasant, mutually rewarding relationship.

When the puppy is two to three months old, secure a flat, narrow leather collar and have him start wearing it (never use a harness, which will encourage tugging and pulling). After a week or so, attach a light leather lead to the collar during play sessions and let the puppy walk around, dragging the lead behind him. Then start holding the end of the lead and coaxing the puppy to come to you. He will then be fully accustomed to collar and lead when you start taking him outside while he is being housebroken.

Housebreaking can be accomplished in a matter of approximately two weeks provided you wait until the dog is mature enough to have some control over bodily functions. This is usually at about four months. Until that time, the puppy should spend most of his day confined to his penned area, with the floor covered with several thicknesses of newspapers so that he may relieve himself when necessary without damage to floors.

Either of two methods works well in housebreaking—the choice depending upon where you live. If you live in a house with a readily accessible yard, you will probably want to train the puppy from the beginning to go outdoors. If you live in an apartment without easy access to a yard, you may decide to train him first to relieve himself on newspapers and then when he has learned control, to teach the puppy to go outdoors.

If you decide to train the puppy by taking him outdoors, arrange some means of confining him indoors where you can watch him closely—in a small penned area, or tied to a short lead (five or six feet). Dogs are naturally clean animals, reluctant to soil their quarters, and confining the puppy to a limited area will encourage him to avoid making a mess.

A young puppy must be taken out often, so watch your puppy closely and if he indicates he is about to relieve himself, take him out at once. If he has an accident, scold him and take him out so he will associate the act of going outside with the need to relieve himself. Always take the puppy out within an hour after meals—preferably to the same place each time—and make sure he relieves himself before you return him to the house. Restrict his water for two hours before bedtime and take him out just before you retire for the night. When you wake in the morning, take him out again.

For paper training, set aside a particular room and cover a large area of the floor with several thicknesses of newspapers. Confine the dog on a short leash and each time he relieves himself, remove the soiled papers and replace them with clean ones.

As his control increases, gradually decrease the paper area, leaving part of the floor bare. If he uses the bare floor, scold him mildly and put him on the papers, letting him know that there is where he is to relieve himself. As he comes to understand the idea, increase the bare area until papers cover only space equal to approximately two full newspaper sheets. Keep him using the papers, but begin taking him out on a leash at the times of day that he habitually relieves himself. Watch him closely when he is indoors and at the first sign that he needs to go, take him outdoors. With this method too, restrict the puppy's water for two hours before bedtime, but if necessary, permit him to use the papers before you retire for the night.

Using either method, the puppy will be housebroken in an amazingly short time. Once he has learned control he will need to relieve himself only four or five times a day.

Informal obedience training, started at the age of about six to eight months, will provide a good background for any advanced training you may decide to give your dog later. The collar most effective for training is the metal chain-link variety. The correct size for your dog will be about one inch longer than the measurement around the largest part of his head. The chain must be slipped through one of the rings so the collar forms a loop. The collar should be put on with the loose ring at the right of the dog's neck, the chain attached to it coming over the neck and through the holding ring, rather than under the neck. Since the dog is to be at your left for most of the training, this makes the collar most effective.

The leash should be attached to the loose ring, and should be either webbing or leather, six feet long and a half inch to a full inch

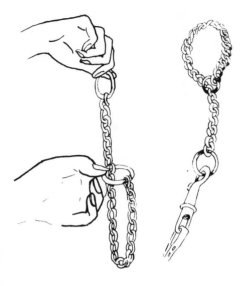

Chain-link collar. The collar should be removed whenever the dog is not under your immediate supervision, for many dogs have met death by strangulation when a collar was left on and became entangled in some object.

wide. When you want your dog's attention, or wish to correct him, give a light, quick pull on the leash, which will momentarily tighten the collar about the neck. Release the pressure instantly, and the correction will have been made. If the puppy is already accustomed to a leather collar, he will adjust easily to the training collar. But before you start training sessions, practice walking with the dog until he responds readily when you increase tension on the leash.

Set aside a period of fifteen minutes, once or twice a day, for regular training sessions, and train in a place where there will be no distractions. Teach only one exercise at a time, making sure the dog has mastered it before going on to another. It will probably take at least a week for the dog to master each exercise. As training progresses, start each session by reviewing exercises the dog has already learned, then go on to the new exercise for a period of concerted practice. When discipline is required, make the correction immediately, and always praise the dog after corrections as well as when he obeys promptly. During each session stick strictly to business. Afterwards, take time to play with the dog.

The first exercise to teach is heeling. Have the dog at your left and hold the leash as shown in the illustration on the preceding page. Start walking, and just as you put your foot forward for the first step, say your dog's name to get his attention, followed by the command, "Heel!" Simultaneously, pull on the leash lightly. As you walk, try to keep the dog at your left side, with his head alongside your left leg. Pull on the leash as necessary to urge him forward or back, to right or left, but keep him in position. Each time you pull on the leash, say "Heel!" and praise the dog lavishly. When the dog heels properly in a straight line, start making circles, turning corners, etc.

Once the dog has learned to heel well, start teaching the "sit." Each time you stop while heeling, command "Sit!" The dog will be at your left, so use your left hand to press on his rear and guide him to a sitting position, while you use the leash in your right hand to keep his head up. Hold him in position for a few moments while you praise him, then give the command to heel. Walk a few steps, stop, and repeat the procedure. Before long he will automatically sit whenever you stop. You can then teach the dog to "sit" from any position.

When the dog will sit on command without correction, he is ready to learn to stay until you release him. Simply sit him, command "Stay!" and hold him in position for perhaps half a minute, repeating "Stay," if he attempts to stand. You can release him by saying "O.K." Gradually increase the time until he will stay on command for three or four minutes.

The "stand-stay" should also be taught when the dog is on leash. While you are heeling, stop and give the command "Stand!" Keep the dog from sitting by quickly placing your left arm under him, immediately in front of his right hind leg. If he continues to try to sit, don't scold him but start up again with the heel command, walk a few steps, and stop again, repeating the stand command and preventing the dog from sitting. Once the dog has mastered the stand, teach him to stay by holding him in position and repeating the word "Stay!"

The "down stay" will prove beneficial in many situations, but especially if you wish to take your dog in the car without confining him to a crate. To teach the "down," have the dog sitting at your side with collar and leash on. If he is a large dog, step forward with the leash in your hand and turn so you face him. Let the leash touch the floor, then step over it with your right foot so it is under the instep of your shoe. Grasping the leash low down with both hands, slowly pull up, saying, "Down!" Hold the leash taut until the dog goes down. Once he responds well, teach the dog to stay in the down position (the down-stay), using the same method as for the sit- and stand-stays.

To teach small dogs the "down," another method may be used. Have the dog sit at your side, then kneel beside him. Reach across his back with your left arm, and take hold of his left front leg close to the body. At the same time, with your right hand take hold of his right front leg close to his body. As you command "Down!" gently lift the legs and place the dog in the down position. Release your hold on his legs and slide your left hand onto his back, repeating, "Down, stay," while keeping him in position.

The "come" is taught when the dog is on leash and heeling. Simply walk along, then suddenly take a step backward, saying "Come!" Pull the leash as you give the command and the dog will turn and follow you. Continue walking backward, repeatedly saying "Come," and tightening the leash if necessary.

Once the dog has mastered the exercises while on leash, try taking the leash off and going through the same routine, beginning with the heeling exercise. If the dog doesn't respond promptly, he needs review with the leash on. But patience and persistence will be rewarded, for you will have a dog you can trust to respond promptly under all conditions.

Even after they are well trained, dogs sometimes develop bad habits that are hard to break. Jumping on people is a common habit, and all members of the family must assist if it is to be broken. If the dog is a large or medium breed, take a step forward and raise your knee just as he starts to jump on you. As your knee strikes the dog's chest, command "Down!" in a scolding voice. When a small dog jumps on you, take both front paws in your hands, and, while talking in a pleasant tone of voice, step on the dog's back feet just hard enough to hurt them slightly. With either method the dog is taken by surprise and doesn't associate the discomfort with the person causing it.

Occasionally a dog may be too chummy with guests who don't care for dogs. If the dog has had obedience training, simply command "Come!" When he responds, have him sit beside you.

Excessive barking is likely to bring complaints from neighbors, and persistent efforts may be needed to subdue a dog that barks without provocation. To correct the habit, you must be close to the dog when he starts barking. Encircle his muzzle with both hands, hold his mouth shut, and command "Quiet!" in a firm voice. He should soon learn to respond so you can control him simply by giving the command.

Sniffing other dogs is an annoying habit. If the dog is off leash and sniffs other dogs, ignoring your commands to come, he needs

111

Benching area at Westminster Kennel Club Show.

to review the lessons on basic behavior. When the dog is on leash, scold him, then pull on the leash, command "Heel," and walk away from the other dog.

A well-trained dog will be no problem if you decide to take him with you when you travel. No matter how well he responds, however, he should never be permitted off leash when you walk him in a strange area. Distractions will be more tempting, and there will be more chance of his being attacked by other dogs. So whenever the dog travels with you, take his leash along—and use it.

Judging for Best in Show at Westminster Kennel Club Show.

Show Competition

Centuries ago, it was common practice to hold agricultural fairs in conjunction with spring and fall religious festivals, and to these gatherings, cattle, dogs, and other livestock were brought for exchange. As time went on, it became customary to provide entertainment, too. Dogs often participated in such sporting events as bull baiting, bear baiting, and ratting. Then the dog that exhibited the greatest skill in the arena was also the one that brought the highest price when time came for barter or sale. Today, these fairs seem a far cry from our highly organized bench shows and field trials. But they were the forerunners of modern dog shows and played an important role in shaping the development of purebred dogs.

The first organized dog show was held at Newcastle, England, in 1859. Later that same year, a show was held at Birmingham. At both shows dogs were divided into four classes and only Pointers and Setters were entered. In 1860, the first dog show in Germany was held at Apoldo, where nearly one hundred dogs were exhibited and entries were divided into six groups. Interest expanded rapidly, and by the time the Paris Exhibition was held in 1878, the dog show was a fixture of international importance.

In the United States, the first organized bench show was held in 1874 in conjunction with the meeting of the Illinois State Sportsmen's Association in Chicago, and all entries were dogs of sporting breeds. Although the show was a rather casual affair, interest spread quickly. Before the end of the year, shows were held in Oswego, New York, Mineola, Long Island, and Memphis, Tennessee. And the latter combined a bench show with the first organized field trial ever held in the United States. In January 1875, an all-breed show (the first in the United States) was held at Detroit, Michigan. From then on, interest increased rapidly, though rules were not always uniform, for there was no organization through which to coordinate activities until September 1884 when The American Kennel Club was founded. Now the largest dog registering organization in the world, the AKC is an association of several hundred member clubs—all breed, specialty, field trial, and obedience groups—each represented by a delegate to the AKC.

The several thousand shows and trials held annually in the United States do much to stimulate interest in breeding to produce better looking, sounder, purebred dogs. For breeders, shows provide a means of measuring the merits of their work as compared with accomplishments of other breeders. For hundreds of thousands of dog fanciers, they provide an absorbing hobby.

Bench Shows

At bench (or conformation) shows, dogs are rated comparatively on their physical qualities (or conformation) in accordance with breed Standards which have been approved by The American Kennel Club. Characteristics such as size, coat, color, placement of eye or ear, general soundness, etc., are the basis for selecting the best dog in a class. Only purebred dogs are eligible to compete and if the show is one where points toward a championship are to be awarded, a dog must be at least six months old.

Bench shows are of various types. An all-breed show has classes for all of the breeds recognized by The American Kennel Club as well as a Miscellaneous Class for breeds not recognized, such as the Australian Cattle Dog, the Ibizan Hound, the Spinoni Italiani, etc. A sanctioned match is an informal meeting where dogs compete but not for championship points. A specialty show is confined to a single breed. Other shows may restrict entries to champions of record, to American-bred dogs, etc. Competition for Junior Showmanship or for Best Brace, Best Team, or Best Local Dog may be included. Also, obedience competition is held in conjunction with many bench shows.

The term "bench show" is somewhat confusing in that shows of this type may be either "benched" or "unbenched." At the former, each dog is assigned an individual numbered stall where he must remain throughout the show except for times when he is being judged, groomed, or exercised. At unbenched shows, no stalls are provided and dogs are kept in their owners' cars or in crates when not being judged.

A show where a dog is judged for conformation actually constitutes an elimination contest. To begin with, the dogs of a single breed compete with others of their breed in one of the regular classes: Puppy, Novice, Bred by Exhibitor, American-Bred, or

Open, and, finally, Winners, where the top dogs of the preceding five classes meet. The next step is the judging for Best of Breed (or Best of Variety of Breed). Here the Winners Dog and Winners Bitch (or the dog named Winners if only one prize is awarded) compete with any champions that are entered, together with any undefeated dogs that have competed in additional non-regular classes. The dog named Best of Breed (or Best of Variety of Breed), then goes on to compete with the other Best of Breed winners in his Group. The dogs that win in Group competition then compete for the final and highest honor, Best in Show.

When the Winners Class is divided by sex, championship points are awarded the Winners Dog and Winners Bitch. If the Winners Class is not divided by sex, championship points are awarded the dog or bitch named Winners. The number of points awarded varies, depending upon such factors as the number of dogs competing, the Schedule of Points established by the Board of Directors of the AKC, and whether the dog goes on to win Best of Breed, the Group, and Best in Show.

In order to become a champion, a dog must win fifteen points, including points from at least two major wins—that is, at least two shows where three or more points are awarded. The major wins must be under two different judges, and one or more of the remaining points must be won under a third judge. The most points ever awarded at a show is five and the least is one, so, in order to become a champion, a dog must be exhibited and win in at least three shows, and usually he is shown many times before he wins his championship.

Pure Bred Dogs—American Kennel Gazette and other dog magazines contain lists of forthcoming shows, together with names and addresses of sponsoring organizations to which you may write for entry forms and information relative to fees, closing dates, etc. Before entering your dog in a show for the first time, you should familiarize yourself with the regulations and rules governing competition. You may secure such information from The American Kennel Club or from a local dog club specializing in your breed. It is essential that you also familiarize yourself with the AKC approved Standard for your breed so you will be fully aware of characteristics worthy of merit as well as those considered faulty, or possibly even serious enough to disqualify the dog from competition. For instance, monorchidism (failure of one testicle to descend) and cryptorchidism (failure of both testicles to descend) are disqualifying faults in all breeds.

If possible, you should first attend a show as a spectator and observe judging procedures from ringside. It will also be helpful to join a local breed club and to participate in sanctioned matches before entering an all-breed show.

The dog should be equipped with a narrow leather show lead and a show collar—never an ornamented or spiked collar. For benched shows, either a bench crate or a metal-link bench chain to fasten the dog to the bench will be needed. For unbenched shows, the dog's crate should be taken along so that he may be confined in comfort when he is not appearing in the ring. A dog should never be left in a car with all the windows closed. In hot weather the temperature will become unbearable in a very short time. Heat exhaustion may result from even a short period of confinement, and death may ensue.

Food and water dishes will be needed, as well as a supply of the food and water to which the dog is accustomed. Brushes and combs are also necessary, so that you may give the dog's coat a final grooming after you arrive at the show.

Familiarize yourself with the schedule of classes ahead of time, for the dog must be fed and exercised and permitted to relieve himself, and any last-minute grooming completed before his class is called. Both you and the dog should be ready to enter the ring unhurriedly. A good deal of skill in conditioning, training, and handling is required if a dog is to be presented properly. And it is essential that the handler himself be composed, for a jittery handler will transmit his nervousness to his dog.

Once the class is assembled in the ring, the judge will ask that the dogs be paraded in line, moving counter-clockwise in a circle. If you have trained your dog well, you will have no difficulty controlling him in the ring, where he must change pace quickly and gracefully and walk and trot elegantly and proudly with head erect. The show dog must also stand quietly for inspection, posing like a statue for several minutes while the judge observes his structure in detail, examines teeth, feet, coat, etc. When the judge calls your dog forward for individual inspection, do not attempt to converse, but answer any questions he may ask.

As the judge examines the class, he measures each dog against the ideal described in the Standard, then measures the dogs against each other in a comparative sense and selects for first place the dog that comes closest to conforming to the Standard for its breed. If your dog isn't among the winners, don't grumble. If he places first, don't brag loudly. For a bad loser is disgusting, but a poor winner is insufferable.

Junior Showmanship Competition at Westminster Kennel Club Show.

Bench crate.   Wagon crate.

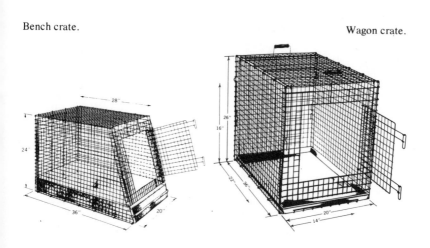

Collars. At the top are two "pinch" or "spiked" collars that are not permitted in AKC shows. Below are two permissible "choke" collars, the one on the right of steel chain and the one on the left of braided nylon. While the choke collars are permitted in conformation shows, they are used more often in obedience competition.

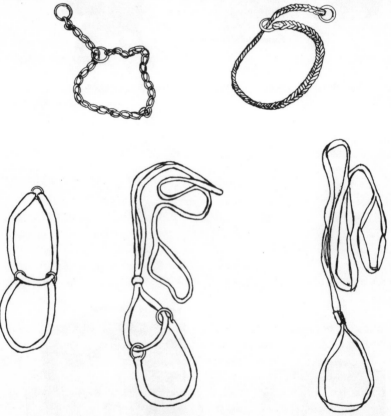

Left, "English" or "Martingale" collar to which lead would be attached. Center, "English" or "Martingale" collar and lead. In using either of these, the dog's head would be inserted through the lower loop. Right, nylon slip lead. Collars and leads of these three types are preferred for conformation showing because they give better control for stacking a dog than the "choke" collars.

Obedience Competition

For hundreds of years, dogs have been used in England and Germany in connection with police and guard work, and their working potential has been evaluated through tests devised to show agility, strength, and courage. Organized training has also been popular with English and German breeders for many years, although it was first practiced primarily for the purpose of training large breeds in aggressive tactics.

There was little interest in obedience training in the United States until 1933 when Mrs. Whitehouse Walker returned from England and enthusiastically introduced the sport. Two years later, Mrs. Walker persuaded The American Kennel Club to approve organized obedience activities and to assume jurisdiction over obedience rules. Since then, interest has increased at a phenomenal rate, for obedience competition is not only a sport the average spectator can follow readily, but also a sport for which the average owner can train his own dog easily. Obedience competition is suitable for all breeds. Furthermore, there is no limit to the number of dogs that may win in competition, for each dog is scored individually on the basis of a point rating system.

The dog is judged on his response to certain commands, and if he gains a high enough score in three successive trials under different judges, he wins an obedience degree. Degrees awarded are "CD"—Companion Dog; "CDX"—Companion Dog Excellent; and "UD"—Utility Dog. A fourth degree, the "TD" or Tracking Dog degree, may be won at any time and tests for it are held apart from dog shows. The qualifying score is a minimum of 170 points out of a possible total of 200, with no score in any one exercise less than 50% of the points allotted.

Since obedience titles are progressive, earlier titles (with the exception of the tracking degree) are dropped as a dog acquires the next higher degree. If an obedience title is gained in another country in addition to the United States, that fact is signified by the word "International," followed by the title.

Trials for obedience trained dogs are held at most of the larger bench shows, and obedience training clubs are to be found in almost all communities today. Information concerning forthcoming trials and lists of obedience training clubs are included regularly in *Pure Bred Dogs–American Kennel Gazette*—and other dog magazines. Pamphlets containing rules and regulations governing obedience competition are available upon request from The American Kennel Club, 51 Madison Avenue, New York, N.Y. 10010. Rules are revised occasionally, so if you are interested in participating in obedience competition, you should be sure your copy of the regulations is current.

All dogs must comply with the same rules, although in broad jump, high jump, and bar jump competition, the jumps are adjusted to the size of the breed. Classes at obedience trials are divided into Novice (A and B), Open (A and B), and Utility (which may be divided into A and B, at the option of the sponsoring club and with the approval of The American Kennel Club).

The Novice class is for dogs that have not won the title Companion Dog. In Novice A, no person who has previously handled a dog that has won a CD title in the obedience ring at a licensed or member trial, and no person who has regularly trained such a dog, may enter or handle a dog. The handler must be the dog's owner or a member of the owner's immediate family. In Novice B, dogs may be handled by the owner or any other person.

The Open A class is for dogs that have won the CD title but have not won the CDX title. Obedience judges and licensed handlers may not enter or handle dogs in this class. Each dog must be handled by the owner or by a member of his immediate family. The Open B class is for dogs that have won the title CD or CDX. A dog may continue to compete in this class after it has won the title UD. Dogs in this class may be handled by the owner or any other person.

The Utility class is for dogs that have won the title CDX. Dogs that have won the title UD may continue to compete in this class, and dogs may be handled by the owner or any other person. Provided the AKC approves, a club may choose to divide the Utility class into Utility A and Utility B. When this is done, the Utility A class is for dogs that have won the title CDX and have not won the title UD. Obedience judges and licensed handlers may not enter or handle dogs in this class. All other dogs that are eligible for the Utility class but not eligible for Utility A may be entered in Utility B.

Novice competition includes such exercises as heeling on and off lead, the stand for examination, coming on recall, and the long sit and the long down.

In Open competition, the dog must perform such exercises as heeling free, the drop on recall, and the retrieve on the flat and over the high jump. Also, he must execute the broad jump, and the long sit and long down.

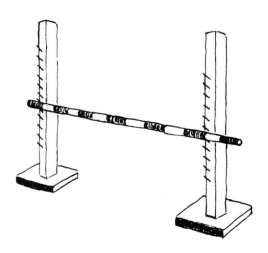

Bar Jump.

In the Utility class, competition includes scent discrimination, the directed retrieve, the signal exercise, directed jumping, and the group examination.

Tracking is the most difficult test. It is always done out-of-doors, of course, and, for obvious reasons, cannot be held at a dog show. The dog must follow a scent trail that is about a quarter mile in length. He is also required to find a scent object (glove, wallet, or other article) left by a stranger who has walked the course to lay down the scent. The dog is required to follow the trail a half to two hours after the scent is laid.

An ideal way to train a dog for obedience competition is to join an obedience class or a training club. In organized class work, beginners' classes cover pretty much the same exercises as those described in the chapter on manners. However, through class work you will develop greater precision than is possible in training your dog by yourself. Amateur handlers often cause the dog to be penalized, for if the handler fails to abide by the rules, it is the dog that suffers the penalty. A common infraction of the rules is using more than one signal or command where regulations stipulate only one may be used. Classwork will help eliminate such errors, which the owner may make unconsciously if he is working alone. Working with a class will also acquaint both dog and handler with ring procedure so that obedience trials will not present unforeseen problems.

Thirty or forty owners and dogs often comprise a class, and exercises are performed in unison, with individual instruction provided if it is required. The procedure followed in training—in fact, even wording of various commands—may vary from instructor to instructor. Equipment used will vary somewhat, also, but will usually include a training collar and leash, a long line, a dumbbell, and a jumping stick. The latter may be a short length of heavy doweling or a broom handle and both it and the dumbbell are usually painted white for increased visibility.

A bitch in season must never be taken to a training class, so before enrolling a female dog, you should determine whether she may be expected to come into season before classes are scheduled to end. If you think she will, it is better to wait and enroll her in a later course, rather than start the course and then miss classes for several weeks.

In addition to the time devoted to actual work in class, the dog must have regular, daily training sessions for practice at home. Before each class or home training session, the dog should be exercised so he will not be highly excited when the session starts, and he must be given an opportunity to relieve himself before the session begins. (Should he have an accident during the class, it is your responsibility to clean up after him.) The dog should be fed several hours before time for the class to begin or else after the class is over—never just before going to class.

If you decide to enter your dog in obedience competition, it is well to enter a small, informal show the first time. Dogs are usually called in the order in which their names appear in the catalog, so as soon as you arrive at the show, acquaint yourself with the schedule. If your dog is not the first to be judged, spend some time at ringside, observing the routine so you will know what to expect when your dog's turn comes.

In addition to collar, leash, and other equipment, you should take your dog's food and water pans and a supply of the food and water to which he is accustomed. You should also take his brushes and combs in order to give him a last-minute brushing before you enter the ring. It is important that the dog look his best even though he isn't to be judged on his appearance.

Before entering the ring, exercise your dog, give him a drink of water, and permit him to relieve himself. Once your dog enters the ring, give him your full attention and be sure to give voice commands distinctly so he will hear and understand, for there will be many distractions at ringside.

Dumbbells.

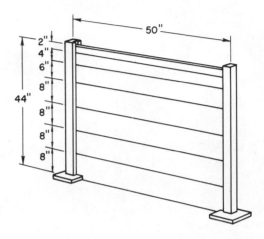

Solid hurdle.

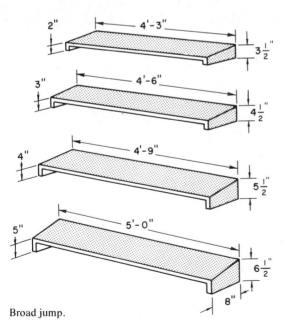

Broad jump.

Top dogs in Utility Class. This illustrates the variety of breeds that compete in obedience.

Genetics

Genetics, the science of heredity, deals with the processes by which physical and mental traits of parents are transmitted to offspring. For centuries, man has been trying to solve these puzzles, but only in the last two hundred years has significant progress been made.

During the eighteenth century, Kölreuter, a German scientist, made revolutionary discoveries concerning plant sexuality and hybridization but was unable to explain just how hereditary processes worked. In the middle of the nineteenth century, Gregor Johann Mendel, an Augustinian monk, experimented with the ordinary garden pea and made other discoveries of major significance. He found that an inherited characteristic was inherited as a complete unit, and that certain characteristics predominated over others. Next, he observed that the hereditary characteristics of each parent are contained in each offspring, even when they are not visible, and that "hidden" characteristics can be transferred without change in their nature to the grandchildren, or even later generations. Finally, he concluded that although heredity contains an element of uncertainty, some things are predictable on the basis of well-defined mathematical laws.

Unfortunately, Mendel's published paper went unheeded, and when he died in 1884 he was still virtually unknown to the scientific world. But other researchers were making discoveries, too. In 1900, three different scientists reported to learned societies that much of their research in hereditary principles had been proved years before by Gregor Mendel and that findings matched perfectly.

Thus, hereditary traits were proved to be transmitted through the chromosomes found in pairs in every living being, one of each pair contributed by the mother, the other by the father. Within each chromosome have been found hundreds of smaller structures, or genes, which are the actual determinants of hereditary characteristics. Some genes are dominant and will be seen in the offspring. Others are recessive and will not be outwardly apparent, yet can be passed on to the offspring to combine with a similar recessive gene of the other parent and thus be seen. Or they may be passed on to the offspring, not be outwardly apparent, but be passed on again to become apparent in a later generation.

Once the genetic theory of inheritance became widely known, scientists began drawing a well-defined line between inheritance and environment. More recent studies show some overlapping of these influences and indicate a combination of the two may be responsible for certain characteristics. For instance, studies have proved that extreme cold increases the amount of black pigment in the skin and hair of the "Himalayan" rabbit, although it has little or no effect on the white or colored rabbit. Current research also indicates that even though characteristics are determined by the genes, some environmental stress occurring at a particular period of pregnancy might cause physical change in the embryo.

Long before breeders had any knowledge of genetics, they practiced one of its most important principles—selective breeding. Experience quickly showed that "like begets like," and by breeding like with like and discarding unlike offspring, the various individual breeds were developed to the point where variations were relatively few. Selective breeding is based on the idea of maintaining the quality of a breed at the highest possible level, while improving whatever defects are prevalent. It requires that only the top dogs in a litter be kept for later breeding, and that inferior specimens be ruthlessly eliminated.

In planning any breeding program, the first requisite is a definite goal—that is, to have clearly in mind a definite picture of the type of dog you wish eventually to produce. To attempt to breed perfection is to approach the problem unrealistically. But if you don't breed for improvement, it is preferable that you not breed at all.

As a first step, you should select a bitch that exemplifies as many of the desired characteristics as possible and mate her with a dog that also has as many of the desired characteristics as possible. If you start with mediocre pets, you will produce mediocre pet puppies. If you decide to start with more than one bitch, all should closely approach the type you desire, since you will then stand a better chance of producing uniformly good puppies from all. Breeders often start with a single bitch and keep the best bitches in every succeeding generation.

Experienced breeders look for "prepotency" in breeding stock—that is, the ability of a dog or bitch to transmit traits to most or all of its offspring. While the term is usually used to describe the transmission of good qualities, a dog may also be prepotent in

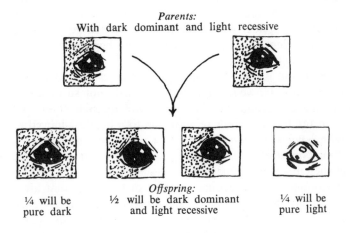

Parents:
One pure dark eyes
and one pure light eyes

Dark eyes   Light eyes

Offspring:
Eyes dark (dominant) with light recessive

Parents:
With dark dominant and light recessive

Offspring:

¼ will be   ½ will be dark dominant   ¼ will be
pure dark   and light recessive   pure light

The above is a schematic representation of the Mendelian law as it applies to the inheritance of eye color. The law applies in the same way to the inheritance of other physical characteristics.

transmitting faults. To be prepotent in a practical sense, a dog must possess many characteristics controlled by dominant genes. If desired characteristics are recessive, they will be apparent in the offspring only if carried by both sire and dam. Prepotent dogs and bitches usually come from a line of prepotent ancestors, but the mere fact that a dog has exceptional ancestors will not necessarily mean that he himself will produce exceptional offspring.

A single dog may sire a tremendous number of puppies, whereas a bitch can produce only a comparatively few litters during her lifetime. Thus, a sire's influence may be very widespread as compared to that of a bitch. But in evaluating a particular litter, it must be remembered that the bitch has had as much influence as has had the dog.

Inbreeding, line-breeding, outcrossing, or a combination of the three are the methods commonly used in selective breeding.

Inbreeding is the mating together of closely related animals, such as father-daughter, mother-son, or brother-sister. Although some breeders insist such breeding will lead to the production of defective individuals, it is through rigid inbreeding that all breeds of dogs have been established. Controlled tests have shown that any harmful effects appear within the first five or ten generations, and that if rigid selection is exercised from the beginning, a vigorous inbred strain will be built up.

Line-breeding is also the mating together of individuals related by family lines. However, matings are made not so much on the basis of the dog's and bitch's relationship to each other, but, instead, on the basis of their relationship to a highly admired ancestor, with a view to perpetuating that ancestor's qualities. Line-breeding constitutes a long-range program and cannot be accomplished in a single generation.

Outcrossing is the breeding together of two dogs that are unrelated in family lines. Actually, since breeds have been developed through the mating of close relatives, all dogs within any given breed are related to some extent. There are few breedings that are true outcrosses, but if there is no common ancestor within five generations, a mating is usually considered an outcross.

Experienced breeders sometimes outcross for one generation in order to eliminate a particular fault, then go back to inbreeding or line-breeding. Neither the good effects nor the bad effects of outcrossing can be truly evaluated in a single mating, for undesirable recessive traits may be introduced into a strain, yet not show up for several generations. Outcrossing is better left to experienced

128

breeders, for continual outcrossing results in a wide variation in type and great uncertainty as to the results that may be expected.

Two serious defects that are believed heritable—subluxation and orchidism—should be zealously guarded against, and afflicted dogs and their offspring should be eliminated from breeding programs. Subluxation is a condition of the hip joint where the bone of the socket is eroded and the head of the thigh bone is also worn away, causing lameness which becomes progressively more serious until the dog is unable to walk. Orchidism is the failure of one or both testicles to develop and descend properly. When one testicle is involved, the term "monorchid" is used. When both are involved, "cryptorchid" is used. A cryptorchid is almost always sterile, whereas a monorchid is usually fertile. There is evidence that orchidism "runs in families" and that a monorchid transmits the tendency through bitch and male puppies alike.

Through the years, many misconceptions concerning heredity have been perpetuated. Perhaps the one most widely perpetuated is the idea evolved hundreds of years ago that somehow characteristics were passed on through the mixing of the blood of the parents. We still use terminology evolved from that theory when we speak of bloodlines, or describe individuals as full-blooded, despite the fact that the theory was disproved more than a century ago.

Also inaccurate and misleading is any statement that a definite fraction or proportion of an animal's inherited characteristics can be positively attributed to a particular ancestor. Individuals lacking knowledge of genetics sometimes declare that an individual receives half his inherited characteristics from each parent, a quarter from each grandparent, an eighth from each great-grandparent, etc. Thousands of volumes of scientific findings have been published, but no simple way has been found to determine positively which characteristics have been inherited from which ancestors, for the science of heredity is infinitely complex.

Any breeder interested in starting a serious breeding program should study several of the books on canine genetics and breeding and whelping that are currently available. Two excellent works covering these subjects are *Meisen Breeding Manual,* by Hilda Meisenzahl, and *The Standard Book of Dog Breeding,* by Dr. Alvin Grossman—both published by the publisher of this book.

Whelping box. Detail at right shows proper side-wall construction which helps keep small puppies confined and provides sheltered nook to prevent crushing or smothering.

Breeding and Whelping

The breeding life of a bitch begins when she comes into season the first time at the age of eight to ten months. Thereafter, she will come in season at roughly six-month intervals. Her maximum fertility builds up from puberty to full maturity and then declines until a state of total sterility is reached in old age. Just when this occurs is hard to determine, for the fact that an older bitch shows signs of being in season doesn't necessarily mean she is still capable of reproducing.

The length of the season varies from eighteen to twenty-one days. The first indication is a pronounced swelling of the vulva with coincidental bleeding (called "showing color") for about the first seven to nine days. The discharge gradually turns to a creamy color, and it is during this phase (estrus), from about the tenth to the fifteenth days, that the bitch is ovulating and is receptive to the male. The ripe, unfertilized ova survive for about seventy-two hours. If fertilization doesn't occur, the ova die and are discharged the next time the bitch comes in season. If fertilization does take place, each ovum attaches itself to the walls of the uterus, a membrane forms to seal it off, and a foetus develops from it.

Following the estrus phase, the bitch is still in season until about the twenty-first day and will continue to be attractive to males, although she will usually fight them off as she did the first few days. Nevertheless, to avoid accidental mating, the bitch must be confined for the entire period. Virtual imprisonment is necessary, for male dogs display uncanny abilities in their efforts to reach a bitch in season.

The odor that attracts the males is present in the bitch's urine, so it is advisable to take her a good distance from the house before permitting her to relieve herself. To eliminate problems completely, your veterinarian can prescribe a preparation that will disguise the odor but will not interfere with breeding when the time is right. Many fanciers use such preparations when exhibiting a bitch and find that nearby males show no interest whatsoever. But it is not advisable to permit a bitch to run loose when she has been given a product of this type, for during estrus she will seek the company of male dogs and an accidental mating may occur.

A potential brood bitch, regardless of breed, should have good bone, ample breadth and depth of ribbing, and adequate room in the pelvic region. Unless a bitch is physically mature—well beyond the puppy stage when she has her first season—breeding should be delayed until her second or a later season. Furthermore, even though it is possible for a bitch to conceive twice a year, she should not be bred oftener than once a year. A bitch that is bred too often will age prematurely and her puppies are likely to lack vigor.

Two or three months before a bitch is to be mated, her physical condition should be considered carefully. If she is too thin, provide a rich, balanced diet plus the regular exercise needed to develop strong, supple muscles. Daily exercise on the lead is as necessary for the too-thin bitch as for the too-fat one, although the latter will need more exercise and at a brisker pace, as well as a reduction of food, if she is to be brought to optimum condition. A prospective brood bitch must have had permanent distemper shots as well as rabies vaccination. And a month before her season is due, a veterinarian should examine a stool specimen for worms. If there is evidence of infestation, the bitch should be wormed.

A dog may be used at stud from the time he reaches physical maturity, well on into old age. The first time your bitch is bred, it is well to use a stud that has already proven his ability by having sired other litters. The fact that a neighbor's dog is readily available should not influence your choice, for to produce the best puppies, you must select the stud most suitable from a genetic standpoint.

If the stud you prefer is not going to be available at the time your bitch is to be in season, you may wish to consult your veterinarian concerning medications available for inhibiting the onset of the season. With such preparations, the bitch's season can be delayed indefinitely.

Usually the first service will be successful. However, if it isn't, in most cases an additional service is given free, provided the stud dog is still in the possession of the same owner. If the bitch misses, it may be because her cycle varies widely from normal. Through microscopic examination, a veterinarian can determine exactly when the bitch is entering the estrus phase and thus is likely to conceive.

The owner of the stud should give you a stud-service certificate, providing a four-generation pedigree for the sire and showing the date of mating. The litter registration application is completed only after the puppies are whelped, but it, too, must be signed by the owner of the stud as well as the owner of the bitch. Registration forms may be secured by writing The American Kennel Club.

In normal pregnancy there is visible enlargement of the abdomen by the end of the fifth week. By palpation (feeling with the fingers) a veterinarian may be able to distinguish developing puppies as early as three weeks after mating, but it is unwise for a novice to poke and prod, and try to detect the presence of unborn puppies.

The gestation period normally lasts nine weeks, although it may vary from sixty-one to sixty-five days. If it goes beyond sixty-five days from the date of mating, a veterinarian should be consulted.

During the first four or five weeks, the bitch should be permitted her normal amount of activity. As she becomes heavier, she should be walked on the lead, but strenuous running and jumping should be avoided. Her diet should be well balanced (see page 41), and if she should become constipated, small amounts of mineral oil may be added to her food.

A whelping box should be secured about two weeks before the puppies are due, and the bitch should start then to use it as her bed so she will be accustomed to it by the time puppies arrive. Preferably, the box should be square, with each side long enough so that the bitch can stretch out full length and have several inches to spare at either end. The bottom should be padded with an old cotton rug or other material that is easily laundered. Edges of the padding should be tacked to the floor of the box so the puppies will not get caught in it and smother. Once it is obvious labor is about to begin, the padding should be covered with several layers of spread-out newspapers. Then, as papers become soiled, the top layer can be pulled off, leaving the area clean.

Forty-eight to seventy-two hours before the litter is to be whelped, a definite change in the shape of the abdomen will be noted. Instead of looking barrel-shaped, the abdomen will sag pendulously. Breasts usually redden and become enlarged, and milk may be present a day or two before the puppies are whelped. As the time becomes imminent, the bitch will probably scratch and root at her bedding in an effort to make a nest, and will refuse food and ask to be let out every few minutes. But the surest sign is a drop in temperature of two or three degrees about twelve hours before labor begins.

The bitch's abdomen and flanks will contract sharply when labor actually starts, and for a few minutes she will attempt to expel a puppy, then rest for a while and try again. Someone should stay with the bitch the entire time whelping is taking place, and if she appears to be having unusual difficulties, a veterinarian should be called.

Puppies are usually born head first, though some may be born feet first and no difficulty encountered. Each puppy is enclosed in a separate membranous sac that the bitch will remove with her teeth. She will sever the umbilical cord, which will be attached to the soft, spongy afterbirth that is expelled right after the puppy emerges. Usually the bitch eats the afterbirth, so it is necessary to watch and make sure one is expelled for each puppy whelped. If afterbirth is retained, the bitch may develop peritonitis and die.

The dam will lick and nuzzle each newborn puppy until it is warm and dry and ready to nurse. If puppies arrive so close together that she can't take care of them, you can help her by rubbing the puppies dry with a soft cloth. If several have been whelped but the bitch continues to be in labor, all but one should be removed and placed in a small box lined with clean towels and warmed to about seventy degrees. The bitch will be calmer if one puppy is left with her at all times.

Whelping sometimes continues as long as twenty-four hours for a very large litter, but a litter of two or three puppies may be whelped in an hour. When the bitch settles down, curls around the puppies and nuzzles them to her, it usually indicates that all have been whelped.

The bitch should be taken away for a few minutes while you clean the box and arrange clean padding. If her coat is soiled, sponge it clean before she returns to the puppies. Once she is back in the box, offer her a bowl of warm beef broth and a pan of cool water, placing both where she will not have to get up in order to reach them. As soon as she indicates interest in food, give her a generous bowl of chopped meat to which codliver oil and dicalcium phosphate have been added.

If inadequate amounts of calcium are provided during the period the puppies are nursing, eclampsia may develop. Symptoms are violent trembling, rapid rise in temperature, and rigidity of muscles. Veterinary assistance must be secured immediately, for death may result in a very short time. Treatment consists of massive doses of calcium gluconate administered intravenously, after which symptoms subside in a miraculously short time.

134

For weak or very small puppies, supplemental feeding is often recommended. Any one of three different methods may be used: tube-feeding (with a catheter attached to a syringe), using an eyedropper (this method requires great care in order to avoid getting formula in the lungs), or using a tiny bottle (the "pet nurser" available at most pet supply stores). The commercially prepared puppy formulas are most convenient and are readily obtainable from a veterinarian, who can also tell you which method of administering the formula is most practical in your particular case. It is important to remember that equipment must be kept scrupulously clean. It can be sterilized by boiling, or it may be soaked in a Clorox solution, then washed carefully and dried between feedings.

All puppies are born blind and their eyes open when they are ten to fourteen days old. At first the eyes have a bluish cast and appear weak, and the puppies must be protected from strong light until at least ten days after the eyes open.

To ensure proper emotional development, young dogs should be shielded from loud noises and rough handling. Being lifted by the front legs is painful and may result in permanent injury to the shoulders. So when lifting a puppy, always place one hand under the chest with the forefinger between the front legs, and place the other hand under his bottom.

Flannelized rubber sheeting is an ideal surface for the bottom of the bed for the new puppies. It is inexpensive and washable, and will provide a surface that will give the puppies traction so that they will not slip either while nursing or when learning to walk.

Sometimes the puppies' nails are so long and sharp that they scratch the bitch's breasts. Since the nails are soft, they can be trimmed with ordinary scissors.

At about four weeks of age, formula should be provided. The amount fed each day should be increased over a period of two weeks, when the puppies can be weaned completely. One of the commercially prepared formulas can be mixed according to directions on the container, or formula can be prepared at home in accordance with instructions from a veterinarian. The formula should be warmed to lukewarm, and poured into a shallow pan placed on the floor of the box. After his mouth has been dipped into the mixture a few times, a puppy will usually start to lap formula. All puppies should be allowed to eat from the same pan, but be sure the small ones get their share. If they are pushed aside, feed them separately. Permit the puppies to nurse part of the time, but gradually increase the number of meals of formula. By the

135

time the puppies are five weeks old, the dam should be allowed with them only at night. When they are about six weeks old, they should be weaned completely. Three meals a day are usually sufficient from this time until the puppies are about three months old, when feedings are reduced to two a day. About the time the dog reaches one year of age, feedings may be reduced to one each day. (For further information on this subject, see page 38.)

Once they are weaned, puppies should be given temporary distemper injections every two weeks until they are old enough for permanent inoculations. At six weeks, stool specimens should be checked for worms, for almost without exception, puppies become infested. Specimens should be checked again at eight weeks, and as often thereafter as your veterinarian recommends.

Sometimes owners decide as a matter of convenience to have a bitch spayed or a male castrated. While this is recommended when a dog has a serious inheritable defect or when abnormalities of reproductive organs develop, in sound, normal purebred dogs, spaying a bitch or castrating a male may prove a definite disadvantage. The operations automatically bar dogs from competing in shows as well as precluding use for breeding. The operations are seldom dangerous, but they should not be performed without serious consideration of these facts.